BUSINESS
OBJECTIVES
PAIRWORK

John Bradley and Simon Clarke

Oxford University Press 1997

Oxford University Press
Great Clarendon Street, Oxford OX2 6DP

Oxford New York
Athens Auckland Bangkok Bombay
Buenos Aires Calcutta Cape Town Dar es Salaam
Delhi Florence Hong Kong Istanbul Karachi
Kuala Lumpur Madras Madrid Melbourne
Mexico City Nairobi Paris Singapore
Taipei Tokyo Toronto
and associated companies in
Berlin Ibadan

OXFORD and OXFORD ENGLISH
are trade marks of Oxford University Press

ISBN 0 19 4513963

© Oxford University Press 1997

First published 1997

No unauthorized photocopying

Acknowledgements

Cover illustration
Shireen Nathoo Design

Illustrations
Ian Jackson pp. 31, 74
Simon Smith pp. 27, 67, 68
Technical Graphics Department, OUP p. 73

Photography
Mike Dudley

The authors and publisher are grateful to those who have
given permission to reproduce the following extracts and
adaptations of copyright material:

Adventure Balloons: for advertisement, p. 15;
The Economist: for graphs, pp. 45, 84, all © The Economist
1996; EL Ltd: for advertisement, p. 8; Forte plc: for hotel
logo, pp. 56, 98; Holiday Inn Worldwide: for hotel logo,
pp. 56, 98; Institutional Investor: for job advertisement
pp. 70, 99; McVitie's Group: for information and diagram,
pp. 72, 73; Mitsubishi: for mobile phone advertisement,
p. 21; New Day Ltd: for extracts from *Ventures*, July/August
1996 , pp. 11, 32, 34; Globus Office World plc: for
photographs and diagrams from Office World catalogue,
pp. 19, 20, 93; Oxford City Council Leisure Services: for
advertising poster p. 15; The Oxford Playhouse: for
advertisement, p. 15; Supranational Hotels: for their logo,
pp.14, 80; The Talkhouse: for advertisement, p. 15; The
following companies for their corporate logos, p. 16: Apple
Computer Inc. registered trademark, BASF, The BBC, Canon,
© Eastman Kodak Company 1970 – registered trademark –
used by permission, ICI, Kellogg's, Rice Krispies, and Frosties
are registered trademarks of Kellogg Company, reproduced
by kind permission of Kellogg Company, Levi's, McDonald's
Restaurants Ltd, Michelin, Microsoft, Mitsubishi, Sony; the
following publishers for permission to reproduce the covers
of their books, p. 34: Hodder & Stoughton, John Wiley &
Sons Inc., McGraw-Hill, Pan Books Ltd., and Sidgewick &
Jackson; Doubleday, p. 22: for the Sam Walton photograph.

Although every effort has been made to trace and contact
copyright holders before publication, this has not been
possible in every case. We apologize for any apparent
infringement of copyright and if notified, the publisher will
be pleased to rectify any errors or omissions at the earliest
opportunity.

The authors are grateful to Academia Lacunza, IH, San
Sebastian, for their help and support during the writing of
this book.

Contents

5

Introduction

Using *Business Objectives Pairwork*

Business Objectives Pairwork is designed for low-intermediate level learners. It is a speaking practice activity book which follows the syllabus of *Business Objectives*. It is mainly designed to be used with the Student's Book. However, it can also be used as a resource book for any Business English course at this level. As with the main course book, each unit is free-standing and the activities can be used continuously from start to finish. Yet, using the book in a flexible manner will also enable the teacher to cater for specific language priorities of different learners. *Business Objectives Pairwork* is also designed for one-to-one teaching and telephone classes. Thus, *Business Objectives Pairwork* can be used in three different ways:

- Speaking activities as part of a traditional language course in the classroom.

- One-to-one teaching programmes where the teacher takes on one of the pairwork roles.

- Speaking activities for one-to-one teaching over the telephone. (See below)

Format of units

Business Objectives Pairwork follows the unit structure of the Student's Book and covers the same themes. The shortest activities last about five minutes and concentrate on specific language points. The longer activities can last up to fifteen or twenty minutes, or longer. These longer exercises aim to provide greater fluency practice and are designed to encourage students to express their own ideas and to describe situations and events in their own lives.

Information Files
Many of the activities require students to exchange different sets of information. Role-play notes for one member (Student B) of each pair are provided in numbered files starting on page 79.

Answer Key
Answers are provided, where necessary, in numbered sections at the back, starting on page 109.

Writing
This is a speaking practice book with little writing to do. However, students are frequently asked to take notes in the information exchange activities, for which space is provided in the book. The teacher may choose to exploit these opportunities for further writing practice if it is needed.

Teaching Business English

As in the Student's Book, activities are based on authentic materials, wherever possible. Documentation from real companies has been used to ensure business authenticity and relevance. Activities also involve students relating and discussing their own business experiences and expertise, to ensure that they contribute directly to the course content wherever possible.

Telephone Teaching

Telephone teaching is particularly effective. Most of the activities in this book have been developed with telephone teaching in mind and if using this approach, the following points are important:

- Teacher and student must be comfortable and able to take notes. Clear communication is vital.

- Adequate time should be given to allow students to prepare for each session.

The benefits are numerous:

- Speaking practice is intensive and challenging.

- There is no need for a classroom, thus saving valuable time for busy professionals. Sessions may be conducted from home or from work.

- Telephone skills are essential for most learners of Business English: this method of teaching provides invaluable practice.

- Once initial barriers are down, students often find speaking in English over the telephone less inhibiting.

- Many students benefit more from short and frequent language sessions, than they do from traditional, weekly, longer classes.

| Meeting People

1.1 Business magazine

1 Read the advertisement below. You want to send this magazine to your partner. Complete the form with their details and ask your partner for any information that you don't know.

Would you like to receive Business English?

Business English is a magazine for people learning English for professional purposes and international communication. About three million people are learning English worldwide. We want to be certain that **Business English** is the right magazine for you. We can send you the magazine free for three months. Please answer the questions and return the form below.

What is the main activity of your company?

What is your job title?

What are you responsible for?

How many hours a week do you study English?

How many people are learning English in your company?

When do you speak or write English? Please tick (√) as appropriate.

- Face-to-face communication
- On the telephone
- Communication by fax or e-mail
- Conferences and trade fairs
- General business travel
- Other

Name

Organization

Address

Tel   Fax

Send to: Circulations Manager, **Business English**, 15 James Street, London, w86 6TA

2 Check with your partner that the information is correct.

Example   *So your name is ————— and you work for —————, is that right?*

1.2 Who's who?

One person uses the information below and the other looks at the information in **File 29** on page 91.

Student A

1 You are attending a trade conference with your partner. You have a fax with the names of other delegates and some basic information about each person. Some of the information is missing. Your partner has the missing information. Ask questions to find the missing information.

Who …	… is from … ?
	… works for … ?
	… works in … ?

What nationality is … ?
Where does … work?
Who does … work for?

FAX

To	
From	
Ref	International Trade Conference

Name	From	Company	Based in	Position
John Waite		RTZ		Sales Manager
Reiner Mattner	South Africa		Johannesburg	
	Japan		Tokyo	Sales Director
Chuang Sun	South Korea	Daewoo	Seoul	Finance Director
Angelos Angelidis		Patterson Zochonis		Marketing Manager
Jacinto Sileci	Brazil		São Paulo	

2 You are now at the conference. In pairs, each take the role of one of the people in the fax above. Imagine you are meeting for the first time and act out the conversation with your partner.

Example　**A**　*Hello, I'm* _____ .

　　　　　B　*How do you do? I'm* _____ .

　　　　　　　I work for _____ . *And you?*

　　　　　A　*I* _____ .

I.3 Company structure

One person uses the information below and the other looks at the information in **File 30** on page 92.

Student A

1 Find out from your partner the missing information about TLM PLC.

> Who is the ...?
> Who is responsible for ...?
> Who is in charge of ...?
> What does ... do?
> Who is ... in charge of?

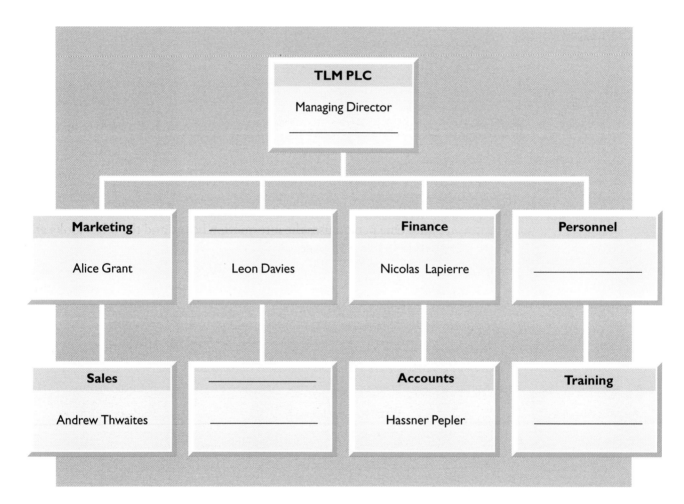

2 Now use the same questions to ask your partner about their company or an imagined one. Use the information to draw an organization chart of the company they describe.

I.4 Do you know...?

I   Complete the first column with notes about a business acquaintance.

	My business acquaintance	My business acquaintance
Name		
Nationality		
Company		
Job/Position		
In charge of		
Lives in		
Travels to work by		
Family		
Interests		

2   Now tell your partner about your friend.

3   Complete the right-hand column with information your partner gives you.

I.5 My business day

Work in pairs. One person uses the information below and the other looks at the information in **File I** on page 79.

Student A

I   You are Marc Taylor, head of the UK Division of 7 Eleven, a food retailer. You are thirty-three. You are responsible for eight hundred employees in fifty-five shops. Below you have notes about a typical day in your life.

Your partner is a journalist for a business magazine. She/he wants to interview you for an article. Use the notes to answer the questions.

> 5.15   Get up.
> 5.30   Exercise for 20 minutes.
> 6.40   Arrive at office, finish work from previous day.
>   Plan schedule for day. Spend morning in office.
>   Phone shops for sales information.
> 2.00   Lunch, sandwich.
> 4.00   Leave office, visit 7 Eleven shops.
> 6.30   Home, relax with friend, watch sport on TV.
> 10.30 Bed.

2   Now interview each other in the same way about your daily routines.

2 Telephoning

2.1 Bingo!

One person uses the grid below and the other looks at the grid in **File 2** on page 79.

Student A

1 This is a fast game. Read the groups of letters to your partner as fast as you can. Say each group once.

YGJ	IEA
WUV	JAE
UJI	GJG
PTY	FAE
HEL	IRT
OWQ	WOW
SQU	TAU

2 Listen to your partner reading out some groups of letters and mark them off in the grid as you hear each one. Now compare your grid with the one in **Key 2.1** on page 109.

2.2 **Which city?**

Write down the names of five different cities in the world. Underline every other letter. Then, without saying the full name, say the underlined letters to your partner. He/she must guess the city. If necessary, give some help.

Example   L __ N __ O __
It's the capital of England.

You	Your partner
1	
2	
3	
4	
5	

2.3 **Telephone language**

1   Look at the following conversation. The speakers don't use the correct language for speaking on the phone. Make the necessary changes, and then practise the conversation with your partner.

A *Galaxy Computers.*

_____

B *I want to speak to Harris.*

_____

A *Who are you?*

_____

B *Johnson.*

_____

A *Who? Repeat your name, please!*

_____

B *Michael Johnson.*

_____

A *Sorry, the line is engaged. Want to wait?*

_____

B *No. Tell him I called, right?*

_____

A *Right.*

_____

Check your dialogue with the one in **Key 2.3**, on page 109.

2.4 Numbers galore

I Put the following conversation into the correct order.

It's TX34B. TX34B. Have you got that?

Yes, of course. Just a minute. Ready?

No, that's all. Bye.

Yes, go ahead.

Could you give me your VAT code number, please.

That's right. Anything else?

Could I just read that back to you? TX34B.

Bye.

I Check the order in **Key 2.4** on page 109. Then practise the conversation with your partner.

2 Now practise similar conversations with your partner. Find out the following:

- Postal code
- Car registration number
- Date of birth
- Identity card number
- Driving licence number
- Fax/telephone number

2.5 Hotel accommodation

One person uses the information below and the other looks at the information in **File 3** on page 80.

Student A

I You are going on a three-day business trip to Seoul, South Korea, for the first time. You have the telephone numbers of two top-class hotels below. Ring each one and ask for information about them using the notes below.

2 Decide which hotel you would like to stay in and then ring the hotel back and make a booking.

	Seoul International Hotel	Seoul Plaza Hotel
	SEOUL INTERNATIONAL HOTEL	SUPRANATIONAL HOTELS
Location		
Transport		
Rooms		
Meetings facilities		
Restaurants and bars		
Prices		
Leisure facilities		
Business centre		
Anything else?		

2.6 Entertaining customers

One person uses the information below and the other looks at the information in **File 4** on page 80.

Student A

1 You work for Rover, a car manufacturer, based in Oxford. You have to entertain six customers from five different countries. Look at these advertisements in the local paper and then phone your partner who works for Effective Business Events, a corporate entertainment company. Use the notes below to find out more information and use the customer profiles to help you make a decision.

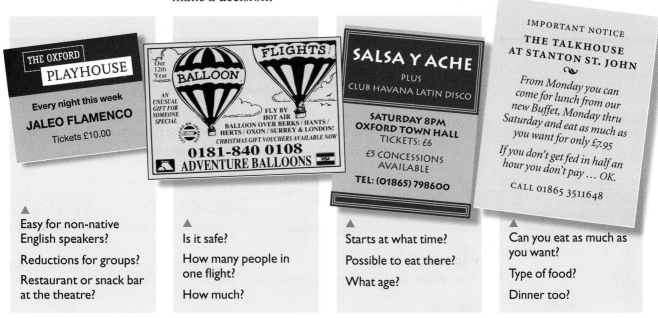

THE OXFORD PLAYHOUSE

Every night this week
JALEO FLAMENCO
Tickets £10.00

BALLOON FLIGHTS!
Our 12th Year
AN UNUSUAL GIFT FOR SOMEONE SPECIAL
FLY BY HOT AIR
BALLOON OVER BERKS / HANTS / HERTS / OXON / SURREY & LONDON!
CHRISTMAS GIFT VOUCHERS AVAILABLE NOW
0181-840 0108
ADVENTURE BALLOONS VISA

SALSA Y ACHE
PLUS
CLUB HAVANA LATIN DISCO
**SATURDAY 8PM
OXFORD TOWN HALL**
TICKETS: £6
£5 CONCESSIONS AVAILABLE
TEL: (01865) 798600

IMPORTANT NOTICE
THE TALKHOUSE AT STANTON ST. JOHN
From Monday you can come for lunch from our new Buffet, Monday thru Saturday and eat as much as you want for only £7.95
If you don't get fed in half an hour you don't pay … OK.
CALL 01865 3511648

▲
Easy for non-native English speakers?

Reductions for groups?

Restaurant or snack bar at the theatre?

▲
Is it safe?

How many people in one flight?

How much?

▲
Starts at what time?

Possible to eat there?

What age?

▲
Can you eat as much as you want?

Type of food?

Dinner too?

CUSTOMER PROFILES

XAVIER ALLENDE
36, Chilean, good English, likes music, and eating local food

TARIQ NASIR
44, Pakistani, fluent English, restaurants and music

ROSANA MENDES
39, Portuguese, good English, likes English food and good music

CHENG WEIQIANG
51, Chinese, excellent English, likes theatre and dancing

HEUNG JYU
38, Korean, very good English, likes eating out, dancing, and listening to music

SAN CHI
42, Korean, English not so good, likes Latin American music, wants to try English food

When you have made a decision, see if you agree with the solution in **Key 2.6** on page 109.

2 **Discussion**

What do you like doing in the evenings? Tell your partner three things that you like doing and three things that you don't like doing.

3 Companies

3.1 Company profiles

1 Choose three companies from the list below but don't say their names. Tell your partner briefly about each company. They must guess the name of the company.

Example **A** *This is a Japanese company. It manufactures a wide range of electronic products such as cameras, printers, and photocopiers.*
               B *Canon.*

When you have finished you can check the details about each company in **Key 3.1** on page 109. These are only suggested answers and you may have more information.

2 Now tell your partner about three companies that you know from your country. Give as much information as possible about each one.

3.2 Checking information 1

When you don't understand parts of a conversation, these are some useful questions you can use.

I'm sorry,	what did you say?
	when did you say?
	where did you say?
	what time/day did you say?
	how many did you say?

What can you say here? Imagine that you don't understand the words in blue. Take it in turns to read the sentences and ask the correct question.

Example **A** *My flight arrives at 5.05.*
B *I'm sorry, what time did you say?*
A *5.05.*

1 The meeting starts at 10.30.
2 The meeting starts at 10.30 on Monday morning.
3 I think about fifteen people are going to the meeting.
4 The meeting is in the Crown Hotel.
5 Mr Ling is going to attend the meeting.
6 The materials cost $150,000.
7 The hotel is about twenty-five kilometres from the airport.
8 I'm sorry, but we can't accept your offer.

Check your answers in **Key 3.2** on page 110.

3.3 Checking information 2

One person uses the information below and the other looks at the information in **File 5** on page 81.

Student A

1 Complete the spaces in the first box with information about any company you know. You can invent a company, if you like. Read your description to your partner as quickly as possible. He/she will check the information by asking questions as you read. When you finish, check that the information is correct.

2 Now listen to your partner and complete the second box with information about your partner's company.

> I'm sorry, what did you say?
> I'm sorry, what do they produce?

Your company

_____ *is a company based in* _____ *in* _____ . *The company employs about* _____ *workers. They produce/provide* _____ *for the* _____ *industry. Their main market is* _____ *and they export to* _____ . *The turnover is about* _____ .

Your partner's company

_____ *is a company based in* _____ *in* _____ . *The company employs about* _____ *workers. They produce/provide* _____ *for the* _____ *industry. Their main market is* _____ *and they export to* _____ . *The turnover is about* _____ .

3.4   **A new factory**

One person uses the information below and the other person looks at the information in **File 39** on page 101.

Student A

1 Your company wants to open a new factory in China. Your partner has information about a new industrial area called the Wuxi-Singapore Industrial Park. You want to know more about it. Prepare the questions to complete the form below.

Name	Wuxi-Singapore Industrial Park
Location	
Travel time to Shanghai	
Airport Port	
Road and rail links	
Companies in the park	
Date of foundation	
No. of companies in area	
Address	
Tel/Fax	

2   **Discussion**

What do you think are the priorities of choosing a new location? Make a list of the five most important things. Compare your list with your partner's.

3.5   **Requesting information**

Student A

You work for Wuxi International Management Services Ltd. Your partner phones you to ask for information about the Wuxi-Singapore Industrial Park. Ask for their details to complete this form.

Please send me further details about the Wuxi-Singapore Industrial Park	
Name	Job title
Company	Type of business
Address	
Tel	Fax
Number of employees	Number of different locations

Student B

You would like to recieve some information about the Wuxi-Singapore Industrial Park in China. Your partner works for the park's management services. Phone and ask him/her to send you some information. Give your personal details and some information about your company. You can invent a company if you wish.

4 Exchanging Information

4.1 Ordering office furniture

One person uses the information below and the other looks at the information in **File 31** on page 93.

Student A
You want to equip a new office with the following furniture.

- A table for a printer
- A filing cabinet
- A large bookshelf
- A stand for a fax machine

Below is a rough plan of the office and a page from the Office World catalogue, a company that supplies office furniture. Ring your partner and ask about prices, dimensions, and colour and make notes in the catalogue. Make sure that they will fit into the office and then place an order for the items you want.

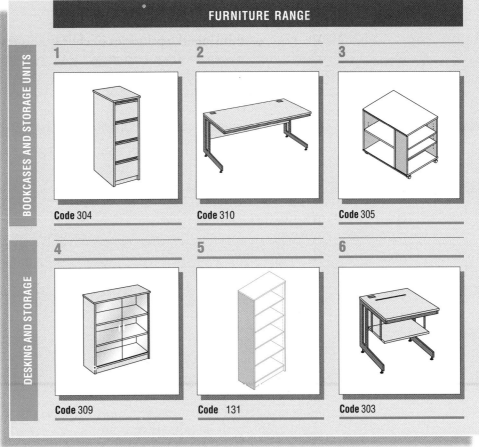

4.2 **Describing objects**

I Look at the office equipment on this page. Choose one and describe it to your partner. Don't say it's name. He/she will try and guess which object you are talking about.

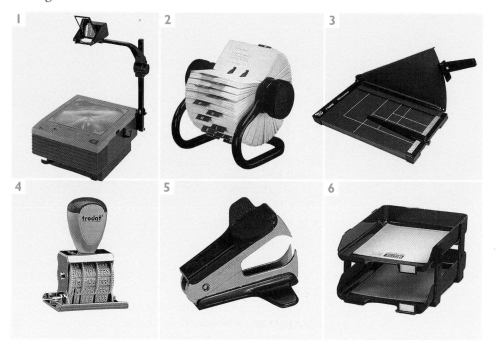

Now take it in turns to describe the other objects.

2 Do you know the names of these objects? Try and guess their names and then check your answers in **Key 4.2** on page 110.

4.3 **Lost property**

I You are at a conference in a small hotel. You have lost something. Go to Reception and explain the problem. Use the conversation below to help you.

A Can I help you?
B *I hope so! I've lost my camera!*
A When did this happen?
B *Just a few minutes ago.*
A Where did you last see it?
B *In the conference room, I think.*
A Could you describe it, please?
B *It's an Olympus. An Olympus 20N. It's a reflex camera.*
A What colour is it?
B *It's black.*
A Is it new?
B *Yes, I bought it last month.*
A OK, just a moment please.

2 Now invent two similar conversations. Use the phrases in blue above but change the words in *italics* if you can.

4.4 A great new invention

Think of an everyday object, and imagine that you invented it, for example, the television, the answering machine, the video camera, the mobile phone, the electronic pocket organiser. Describe it to your partner, who must guess what it is.

Speak about the following:

- name
- size and dimension
- price
- use
- materials
- advantages and disadvantages

Listen to your partner describe an object and using the following questions and comments in response:

> Is it difficult to use?
> When did you get the idea?
> That's quite expensive/cheap!
> That's interesting!
> What a great idea!

4.5 Telesales

One person uses the information below and the other looks at the information in **File 6** on page 81.

Student A

You are a telesales person. Your company sells the Mitsubishi Electric MT-20 mobile phone, pictured below. Phone your partner and try to sell the product, and arrange a demonstration. Try and answer your partner's questions. Don't finish the call until you arrange a demonstration.

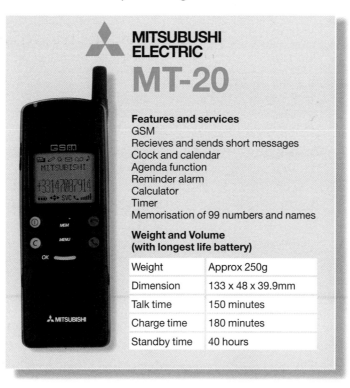

MITSUBUSHI ELECTRIC

MT-20

Features and services
GSM
Recieves and sends short messages
Clock and calendar
Agenda function
Reminder alarm
Calculator
Timer
Memorisation of 99 numbers and names

Weight and Volume (with longest life battery)

Weight	Approx 250g
Dimension	133 x 48 x 39.9mm
Talk time	150 minutes
Charge time	180 minutes
Standby time	40 hours

5 Reporting

5.1 American free enterprise

One person uses the information below and the other looks at the information in **File 32** on page 94.

Student A

1 Read the story about Sam Walton, the world's richest self-made man. Some information is missing. Complete the text by asking your partner questions using the words in the box below.

Sam Walton 1918–1992
A story of American free enterprise

The American entrepreneur, Sam Walton, died in 1992. He had a chain of 1,752 stores across America. His company was worth __1__.

Walton was born in __2__ and studied economics at university. To pay for his studies, he __3__. He then borrowed __4__ and bought a franchise store: the Ben Franklin 'Five and Dime'. When Walton arrived, the store was losing money but soon made a profit with his new ideas.

Walton wanted to start up discount stores across small-town America but the Ben Franklin company disagreed. So with his brother, he opened the first Wal-Mart Discount Store in Arkansas, in __5__. Customers could buy __6__ from jeans to bread.

Walton succeeded because he had a unique style and because he knew how to make money. For example, he learnt to fly a plane and could visit __7__ stores across the USA in a day.

Walton soon built a network of over 1,000 stores, based in __8__. He used the best technology to supply the stores with fresh produce and had a satellite linked to store computers.

Walton died of leukaemia at the age of 74. Today, the Walton family still control Wal-Mart stores. The company has a reputation for friendly service, low prices, and profit-sharing. Wal-Mart's food labels are still called 'Sam's American Choice'.

1 _____	3 _____
2 _____	4 _____

5 _____	7 _____
6 _____	8 _____

How much	When	What	How much
When	How many	Where	How

2 Check your answers with your partner and then look at **Key 5.1**, on page 110, and check that you asked the right questions.

3 Discussion

Do you know any interesting stories about successful entrepreneurs? If you do, tell your partner the story.

5.2 **Rolls-Royce**

One person uses the information below and the other looks at the information in **File 42** on page 104.

Student A

1 Choose the correct verbs from the box below and read the statements about the British car-manufacturing company, Rolls-Royce. Then complete the statements putting the verb into the past tense.

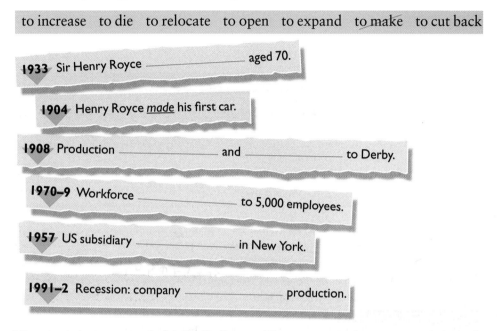

to increase to die to relocate to open to expand to make to cut back

1933 Sir Henry Royce _____ aged 70.

1904 Henry Royce _made_ his first car.

1908 Production _____ and _____ to Derby.

1970–9 Workforce _____ to 5,000 employees.

1957 US subsidiary _____ in New York.

1991–2 Recession: company _____ production.

2 Now imagine you work for Rolls-Royce. You are preparing a presentation of the history of the company. Some of the information is in the wrong order. Exchange the information with your colleague and find the correct order. You both have different sentences.

Example   **B** *What happened first?*
             A *In 1904, Henry Royce made his first car.*
             B *And after that?*

3 Make notes in the table below. Then check the correct order in **Key 5.2** on page 110.

Year	What happened	Year	What happened
1 1904	Henry Royce made his first car.	7	
2		8	
3		9	
4		10	
5		11	
6		12	

4 Now practise giving the presentation with your colleague.

5 Do you know the history of another company? Tell your partner about it.

5.3 Market research

One person uses the information below and the other looks at the information in **File 43** on page 105.

Student A

I You work for Consumer Profile Inc., a market research company based in New York. You are researching the different kinds of holidays taken by business people. Phone your partner and interview him/her using the form below. Make notes below if you wish.

Example *Good morning. I work for Consumer Profile Inc., a market research company. I am researching the different kinds of holidays taken by business people.*

MARKET RESEARCH

HOLIDAY TRENDS IN BUSINESS

Company
Position
No. of holidays per year
Last holiday
When?
Where?
How long?
Who with?
Stayed at?
Travelled by?
Reasons for choice of holiday
First time at this destination?
Holiday good/bad/OK?
Approx. costs
Good value for money?

2 Now change roles. Imagine you are the bank manager. Invent some information and answer your partner's questions.

3 Imagine you are a market-researcher. What subjects interest you? Public transport? Sports shoes? CD Players? Choose a topic with your partner and carry out your own research.

5.4 Making a complaint

One person uses the information below and the other looks at the information in **File 7** on page 81.

Student A

You are the manager in charge of Customer Relations at the Central Hotel, New York. A guest has a complaint. First look at your guest's booking sheet and invoice, and then try to solve the problem.

CENTRAL HOTEL

42nd Street
New York
NY 10541
Tel 809 2323 4561
Fax 809 2323 4560

Invoice Number
3321

INVOICE

Name	Mr David Wynne	
Company	Business Technology Services Ltd	
Room	204	

2 nights double	
2 breakfasts	$300
Mini-bar	$60
Laundry/dry cleaning	$20
Telephone	$30
Fax	$15
	$10

Sub total	$435
Service @ 12%	$52.20
Total	$487.20

FAX

To	Central Hotel New York
From	Business Technology Services
Subject	Booking for Mr David Wynne

This is to confirm a reservation for a single room on the 12th and 13th of this month for Mr David Wynne, Business Technology Services. He arrives at JFK airport in the evening of the 12th but does not want dinner.

Many thanks indeed.

Yours sincerely,

Marion Tyacke

MARION TYACKE

Mini-bar	$20
Laundry	$30
Sub total	$50
Total	**$50**

PAID

5.5 Lost luggage

One person uses the information below and the other looks at the information in **File 40** on page 102.

Student A
Here are two different roles. Read the information and act out the conversations with your partner.

I You arrive at Sydney airport in Australia, on a business trip but your luggage isn't there. Go to the Customer Services Desk and explain your problem. Here are some details.

- A large brown new suitcase.
- Flight QA 306 from Hong Kong.
- You arrived an hour ago.
- One suitcase is left on the carousel. It is very similar to yours.
- Maybe another passenger took your case by mistake.

2 You are the Manager of a travel agency. Your partner has a complaint. Listen and decide what to do. Fill in the form below for your records.

CUSTOMER COMPLAINT

NAME

ADDRESS

TELEPHONE NUMBER

TRAVEL DETAILS

DESTINATION

DETAILS OF COMPLAINT

3 Do you have any similar stories to tell? Describe a bad experience you have had to your partner.

5.6 Restaurant problems

I Look at the picture below and think of four problems that you might have in a restaurant

Example   *Slow service.*

1 _____

2 _____

3 _____

4 _____

2 With your partner, act out four conversations between a customer and the manager of a restaurant. The customer makes a complaint and the manager tries to deal with the problem. Use the problems above and take it in turns to play each role. Use the phrases in the box below.

Can I help you?	Would you like a refund?
What is the problem?	I'm very sorry, but …
I'm afraid …	

6 Socializing

6.1 Invitations

1 Work with your partner and make as many invitations as you can using the words in the chart. Try to use all the boxes.

Example   *Would you like to go to the theatre this evening?*

theatre	tomorrow	this evening	on Saturday	after dinner
golf	this weekend	today	on Tuesday	tomorrow
lunch	with me	tomorrow	today	next week
coffee	before the meeting	now	after lunch	tomorrow morning
sightseeing	tomorrow	this afternoon	this evening	on Sunday
see round/factory	before lunch	now	tomorrow	after the meeting

2 With your partner, decide which invitation(s) produce the following replies.

Example   *I'm afraid I'm having dinner with a customer.*
Would you like to go to the theatre tonight?

1 No thank you, I've just had one.
2 Yes, thank you, could I leave my things in your office?
3 Thank you, but let me invite you.
4 Yes, but I don't play very well.
5 Well, actually, I'd like to have an early night.
6 Yes, I don't know this city very well.
7 I'm sorry, but I'm going to Paris this weekend.
8 Yes, of course. My first meeting after lunch isn't until 5 p.m.

Check **Key 6.1** on page 110 for suggested answers.

3 Make short conversations with your partner. Take it in turns to make your own invitations, and give appropriate replies.

6.2 A social programme

One person uses the information below and the other looks at the information in **File 41** on page 103.

Student A

1 Your partner is visiting your company and is leaving early on Sunday morning. You must entertain him/her on Friday and Saturday. Use the following list of possibilities or make your own suggestions.

- Local restaurant – a good fish place
- Hotel restaurant
- Golf
- Sightseeing
- Football match
- Museum of local history
- Art exhibition
- Theatre and dinner

Make suggestions using expressions from the list below.

> Do you like … ?
> Perhaps we can … ?
> Would you be interested in … ?
> How about … ?
> If you like, we could … ?

2 Now complete the following diary page with your arrangements for this weekend.

FRIDAY	SATURDAY	SUNDAY
		Drive to airport
		Flight BA 573
		Dep. 07.15

6.3 What do you like doing?

1 Read the list of business activities and add your own ideas. What do you like or not like doing? Tick (√) the correct left-hand boxes.

	really enjoy		quite enjoy		don't mind		don't like		can't stand	
driving at night	☐	☐	☐	☐	☐	☐	☐	☐	☐	☐
working at the weekend	☐	☐	☐	☐	☐	☐	☐	☐	☐	☐
working with a computer	☐	☐	☐	☐	☐	☐	☐	☐	☐	☐
travelling on business	☐	☐	☐	☐	☐	☐	☐	☐	☐	☐
flying	☐	☐	☐	☐	☐	☐	☐	☐	☐	☐
giving presentations	☐	☐	☐	☐	☐	☐	☐	☐	☐	☐
lunch with clients	☐	☐	☐	☐	☐	☐	☐	☐	☐	☐
writing reports	☐	☐	☐	☐	☐	☐	☐	☐	☐	☐
staying at hotels	☐	☐	☐	☐	☐	☐	☐	☐	☐	☐
	☐	☐	☐	☐	☐	☐	☐	☐	☐	☐
	☐	☐	☐	☐	☐	☐	☐	☐	☐	☐

2 Discuss the activities with your partner. Put a cross (X) for your partner in the right-hand boxes. Ask him/her lots of questions as in the box below.

Do you like … ?	How do you feel about … ?
Do you enjoy … ?	Why?
What do you feel about … ?	Why not?

6.4 How about meeting for lunch?

1 You receive the two invitations below from your colleague. Read them and choose one that you can accept and one that you cannot accept. Phone and thank your colleague, and give them your answer.

Hello! How are things? I'm coming up to your company on Tuesday next week. How about meeting for lunch? Are you free? Give me a ring and let me know.

The people here at Head Office are organizing a special dinner for the Marketing Manager who's retiring at the end of next month. Can you make it? It's on Friday. Meet at the office at 18.00 if you can. Please let me know.

Thanks for the invitation but …
I'm afraid I'm tied up/busy on …
I'd love to but …
I'd love to.

2 Repeat the activity using the following invitations. This time, change roles with your partner.

Subject:	
Message:	I haven't seen you for ages! Let's play tennis this weekend and you can tell me about all the changes at Head Office. Give me a ring as soon as you can.

Subject:	
Message:	Would you like to come fishing with some friends of mine this weekend? We are leaving at 6 on Saturday morning. Please phone me.

6.5 Requests

I In turns, read the sentences in the picture and give an appropriate response. There may be more than one possibility.

Example **A** *Have a good weekend!*
           B *Thanks. You too.*

2 This time you have a list of responses. Discuss with your partner what the original sentences might be. There will be several possibilities.

Example **A** *I'm sorry to hear that!*
           B *We didn't get the contract.*

1	I'd love to.	4	The same to you.
2	That's great news.	5	I hope so.
3	It doesn't matter; it's not urgent.	6	I'm afraid I'm busy.

Look at **Key 6.5**, 2, on page 110 for suggested answers.

7 Meetings

7.1 A board meeting

One person uses the information below and the other looks at the information in **File 46** on page 108.

Student A

1 Read the article below about a company board meeting in Yorkshire, in the north of England.

MD says: 'Don't Forget Your Rucksack'!

It's the biggest boardroom in the world but there are no tables and no chairs. Larry Gould, Managing Director of the Link Up Group, holds his board meetings in the middle of the Yorkshire countryside.

It's a grey, wet morning in Yorkshire. A group of men and women are walking along a lake. They are laughing and joking. They are wearing boots and waterproof jackets. They look like tourists. But it is Monday, 9am, and they are talking business.

Larry Gould is leading the group. Link Up is a recruitment agency with a turnover of £16 million a year. The others are the board directors and senior managers. This top Yorkshire company is holding a board meeting. Every three months they spend a morning in the countryside, discussing company issues. Gould is certain that these 'board walks' help his management staff to work better.

2 You are the MD of a small manufacturing company. You read the article above in a business magazine and think it's a great idea. Make a list of what, in your opinion, are the advantages and disadvantages of this kind of board meeting.

Advantages	Disadvantages
good for morale	expensive
interesting	waste of valuable time

3 You would like to introduce this kind of meeting into your company. Discuss the article with the Finance Director. Tell him/her your ideas, what you would like to do and why, using some or all of the language in the box below. You must come to an agreement or a compromise.

> What do you think ...?
> I agree/disagree because
> I think we should ...
> Why don't we ...?
> Shall we ...?
> We could ...

4 Now compare your list of advantages and disadvantages with the list in **Key 7.1** on page 111.

7.2 The perfect meeting

What makes a successful meeting? An agenda? A good chairperson? Make a list of proposals to improve meetings in your company. Then discuss your list with your partner.

Make your list here:

- *Prepare an agenda in advance*
-
-
-
-
-
-
-
-
-
-
-
-
-

Compare your list with your partner. Now look at **File 8** on page 81.

7.3 Business books

You and your partner want to buy a leaving present for a colleague. He/she is planning to start their own business. You would like to give some business books and you have a budget of £50. Study the advertisement below and choose some books. Then decide with your colleague which books to buy.

BUSINESS
BOOKS

How to start a small business with very little money; how to win an argument; how to advertise your product; or how to generate new ideas. Here is a selection of interesting books to improve your business skills.

Teach Yourself Copywriting

J. Jonathan Gabay

You've got the best product or service in the world but nobody knows about it. Whatever business you run, this book will teach you how to write good advertising copy to help you market your product.

Hodder & Stoughton
£7.99

Entrepreneurship and Small Firms

David Deakins

This book explains the reality of entrepreneurship in the modern economy. The author looks at the current issues and discusses the problems that entrepreneurs face.

McGraw-Hill
£16.95

Effective Innovation

John Adair

Innovation is essential to the success of any company. In *Effective Innovation*, John Adair looks at creativity and innovation and discusses how to use new ideas in the market place.

Pan Books Ltd.
£6.99

Starting on a Shoestring

Arnold Goldstein

You dream of having your own business, but have very little capital to start off with. *Starting on a Shoestring* is exactly the book for you. Goldstein gives real-world business advice to survive the nineties.

John Wiley & Sons
£12.99

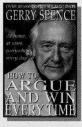

How to Argue and Win Every Time

Gerry Spence

How to Argue and Win Every Time is a book that teaches you how to argue in different situations. Gerry Spence explains how argument is a skill that can be learnt.

Sidgewick & Jackson
£16.99

Company of Heroes

Sims & Manz

The key to managerial success is to create a company of heroes. The authors provide ideas and techniques to help managers become creative and highly motivated leaders.

John Wiley & Sons
£17.99

Glossary
advertising copy a piece of writing to promote a product
entrepreneur a person who starts up a new business
innovation bringing new ideas to a company

7.4 Working conditions

I You are meeting with a colleague to discuss working conditions in your offices. Look at the table below. Think of the advantages and disadvantages and write some ideas in the two columns. Then discuss the proposals with your colleague using the phrases below.

> What do you think about the first proposal?
> I think/I don't think it's a good idea because …

> I think/I don't think we should …
> Do you think we should …?

Present system	Proposal	Advantages	Disadvantages
I Macintosh computers	Change to PC-based system	*Cheaper* *More software*	*Expensive to re-train staff*
2 No staff canteen	Build staff canteen		
3 Working hours 8am-1pm 2pm-5pm	Intensive working day: 7am-3pm (no lunch break)		
4 Executives travel first class	Executives travel tourist class		
5 No bonuses	Bonuses linked to profit		
6 Staff have individual offices	Open plan-offices		
7 Office in city centre	Move to suburbs		

2 Now write out an action plan for each proposal.

Action Plan
I *Change to PC based system*
2
3
4
5
6
7

3 Confirm with your partner the decisions you have made.

Example *So, we're going to change from Macintoshes to a PC-based system.*

7.5 Cutting costs

One person uses the information below and the other looks at the information in **File 33** on page 95.

Student A

Your company, Microtex, produces micro-switches and employs 60 staff. The market is changing rapidly, and the company is introducing expensive technology. To survive, Microtex must make some savings and reduce costs.

You have a meeting with a colleague to discuss the options. Look at the information below. Present the two ideas to your partner. Your partner will then present two more ideas to you. Make notes below. Then decide together which is the best solution.

Remember to consider the following:

- how much money each idea will save
- how each idea will affect productivity
- how to avoid problems with the unions

You must find a solution. If not, the company will go out of business!

Solution	Costs	Savings	Advantages	Disadvantages
Reduce workforce by 10	£500,000 redundancy pay	£100,000 a year	Save money	Lose some good workers
Reduce hours from 40 to 32 hours a week and 20% reduction in pay	No costs but problems with unions could be expensive, strikes	£120,000 a year	Reduce level of production to meet market needs	Opposition from unions, strikes

8 Making Arrangements

8.1 Arranging a meeting

One person uses the information below and the other looks at the information in **File 34** on page 96.

You want a two-hour meeting with your partner and two other people, Mr Harris and Ms Wilson. The meeting is for next Monday or Tuesday. Speak to your partner and find a convenient time. Complete the diary page below. You have lunch from 1.30 to 2.30. When can you have the meeting?

Example   **A** *What are you doing on Tuesday afternoon?*
                    What's Ms Wilson doing on Monday morning?

Diary	You	Mr Harris	Ms Wilson	Your partner
Monday am	meeting with sales people all morning	visit offices of Laker Ltd. London away all morning		
Monday pm	See demonstration of new laser computers			
Tuesday am	Prepare report for board meeting 2 hours	9–11 Inspect new machinery in factory		
Tuesday pm			Personnel Dept meeting all afternoon	

Look at **Key 8.1** on page 111 for the answer.

8.2 Vocabulary

I Complete each space with a word from the box. Compare with your partner.

> fix   cancel   manage   free   suit   tied up   appointment   agenda

1 I'm very sorry but I'm ——————— all next week.

2 11.40 would ——————— me best. Is that all right for you?

3 Good morning. I have an ——————— with Ms Baker at 11.00.

4 I can ——————— Monday morning. What about you?

5 Could we ——————— a time to meet next week?

6 The meeting will finish at 15.00. I'm ——————— after that.

7 Can you put it on the ———————? It's quite important.

8 I'm afraid I have to ——————— our meeting next Tuesday.

Look at **Key 8.2** on page 111 for the answers.

2 Now make short conversations using the sentences above.

Example A *Can I see you sometime next week?*
B *I'm very sorry but I'm tied up next week.*
A *Well, perhaps the following week, it's not urgent*
B *OK. How about Monday morning?*
A *Yes, that's fine.*

Now continue with the rest of the sentences (2–8).

8.3 Organizing your diary

One person uses the information below and the other looks at **File 9** on page 82.

You are a Company Director and your partner is your Personal Assistant. Discuss your appointments for next week and check that the information is correct. The words in blue are your notes and questions.

DAY	AM	PM
MONDAY	Production meeting 09.00? Report?	16.30? Golf match, Tony
TUESDAY	Office lunch. Time? Place?	19.00 Squash match?
WEDNESDAY	Safety Inspection Time? Who is coming?	
THURSDAY	London trip. Transport?	
FRIDAY	09.30 Board Meeting Who is making a presentation? Lunch for directors?	19.30 Theatre Tickets?

8.4 **Sales conference**

1 You and your colleague work for APG Ltd. in Manchester. APG's annual sales conference is next month and you have to prepare the programme. Discuss the documents on pages 40 and 41 and prepare the conference programme, completing the chart below with all the details you can find.

APG LTD	Annual Sales Conference

Venue		Times
Address		Morning session
Dates		
Registration time		Afternoon session

Monday	Opening speech	
	Afternoon session	**Buffet Lunch**
	Speaker	Every day

Tuesday	Morning session	**Buffet Dinner**
	Speaker	Monday
	Afternoon session	
	Speaker	**Coffee Breaks**

Wednesday	Morning session	**Social Events**
	Speaker	Monday
	Afternoon session	
	Speaker	Tuesday

Check your answers in **File 38** on page 100.

2 Now take it in turns to present the programme.

FAX

To   Conference Organizers

From   Lee Anaka

Subject Conference Programme

MESSAGE

This is to remind you that I would like to have the first session on Monday afternoon. My talk will be entitled 'Listening to the Client'. I need approximately two hours, one for the talk and one for discussion and feedback.

Please could you put the UK and European sales targets sessions together on the same day.

I would be grateful for a copy of the programme when it is ready.

Regards

Lee Anaka

LEE ANAKA
European Sales
Manager

I think I am going to need about 3 hours for my session, is this OK? I'd prefer a morning session if possible.

David Strong

I think we need 2 coffee breaks, a half-hour break in the morning and a 15-minute break in the afternoon. The hotel can serve coffee, tea, cakes, and biscuits.
Jane

Urgent message!
David Strong is arriving late, on the Tuesday, at about midday. So don't give him the morning session that day.

Alice

We have arranged a cocktail party for the Monday evening, starting at 7.30 in the hotel reception room. There will, of course, be the main conference dinner on the Tuesday evening at 8 pm in the Devonshire dining room.

Jane

MEMO

FROM Peter Jackson, Head Office APG Ltd.

TO   Conference organizers

RE: Sales conference - opening speech

This is just to remind you that I will be making a short (about 25 minutes) opening speech to the delegates on the Monday to welcome participants and introduce the main speakers.

Peter Jackson

PETER JACKSON
Managing Director

**Annual Sale
Conference
Speakers**

DAVID STRONG	Distribution Probl
PETER JACKSON	Opening speech?
SUSANNAH PETERS	Client Satisfactior
GENEVIÈVE LECLERC	European Sales Ta
LEE ANAKA	Listening to the c
JOHN PEARSON	UK Sales Targets

All conference participants must register between midday and 2 o'clock on Monday the 15th. They must book into their rooms and collect conference documentation before the conference starts at 2.15.

PARK LANE HOTEL

Old Park Lane
London W1V 9FL
TEL: 0171 567 5677
FAX: 0171 009 0909

APG Ltd,
Glencross Lane
Manchester M10

Re: Annual Sales Conference

Dear Sirs,

We would like to confirm the arrangements discussed over the phone today for your annual Sales Conference to be held in our hotel next month.

Dates
Mon 15th   afternoon session only
Tues 16th   morning and afternoon sessions
Weds 17th   morning and afternoon sessions

Participants 50

Times
Mornings   9.30am–1pm
Afternoons 2.15–5pm

Venue
Sessions   The Carlton Room

Buffet lunches Main Dining Room
Monday, Tuesday, and Wednesday (1–2pm)

Buffet dinners Main Dining Room
Monday and Tuesday (6–7pm)

Social events
Cocktail party Reception Room Monday 7.30pm
Conference dinner Devonshire Dining Room Tuesday 8pm

Could you please confirm the above information and would you let me know what time you would like the coffee breaks?

Yours faithfully,

LOUISE CAMPBELL
Business Reservations Manager

8.5 **Business schedule**

One person uses the information below and the other looks at the information in **File 10** on page 82.

1   Look at the following schedule for your business trip to the USA. You are visiting the AXIS company in New York and then going to a trade fair in Boston. You received the schedule last month so there will be some changes. Check the details with your partner who has the latest version and make a note of any changes. Here are some ideas for questions to ask.

> Is my meeting with ... confirmed for ... ?
> Are there any changes to my programme for ... ?
> What's my schedule for ... ?
> Is the date/time still ... ?
> What about my appointment with v ?

2   When you finish, compare notes with your partner and see if you have understood all the changes.

NEW YORK & BOSTON TRIP Provisional Programme

Day One 15th

Flight TWA 234 London to New York
Dep. 12.35   Arr. 19.00
AXIS car at airport,
meet driver at Information Desk
Sheraton Hotel 3 nights
Dinner in hotel 20.00 with Mr Chandler
(Export Manager AXIS)

Day Two 16th

09.00	AXIS car at hotel Visit AXIS offices
09.45	Meet Mr Chandler and Mrs Lawson Discuss new software application
12.45	Lunch with Mrs Lawson
15.00–17.30	Visit software development office
Evening	Opera or theatre trip

Day Three 17th

Morning free	
12.00	AXIS car visit AXIS office
13.00–18.00	Seminar 'Integrated Solutions'
20.00	Dinner with seminar participants

Day Four 18th

07.45	Taxi to airport

Flight Delta Airlines DE 496 New York to Boston
Dep. 09.30   Arr. 11.20
Boston Park Hotel 3 nights

Afternoon	Boston Software 2000 fair Boston Showplace Centre
Visit David Berkley	Mansoft Stand 012-B
Alice Seymour	Delware Stand 343-B
Mary Evans	MCG Stand 213-A
Evening	Free

Days Five and Six 19th,20th

No appointments but try to visit the three companies:
Stock solutions, St-soft, Studio '67

Day Seven 21st

Flight DE 141 Boston–New York–London
Dep. 08.35   Arr. 21.40
Heathrow Hilton Hotel

Day Eight 22nd

08.30	Company car at hotel, return home

9 Describing Trends

9.1 Market indicators

One person uses the information below and the other looks at the information in **File 11** on Page 83.

Student A

1 Look at these statistics. Complete the spaces with the figures in the box. Then check with your partner for the correct figures.

Example   A   *Can I check some information with you? Nickel prices fell below $7,000 a tonne. Is that right?*

               B   *Yes, that's correct.*

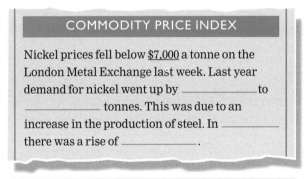

COMMODITY PRICE INDEX

Nickel prices fell below $7,000 a tonne on the London Metal Exchange last week. Last year demand for nickel went up by _____ to _____ tonnes. This was due to an increase in the production of steel. In _____ there was a rise of _____.

12%   ($7,000)   16%   1994   881,000

MEDICAL COSTS

The cost of healthcare is increasing in the West. In OECD* countries, spending on medical goods was just under _____ of GDP in _____. This was about the same as in _____. America is the biggest spender. It spent _____ of its GDP on healthcare in _____. This is more than _____ per person.

1994 $3,500   1993   14.3%   1994   8%

*****OECD** *Organization for Economic Cooperation and Development*

2 Now answer you partner's questions and correct the information, if necessary, using the information below.

> ### MUSIC SALES
>
> Norway spends the most on music. Last year, Norwegians spent US$67 a head on compact discs, records, and cassettes. From 1990 to 1995 sales in Norway rose by 147%. Sales in Japan rose by 148% to $61 per person. America's music industry is the biggest, but sales per person are $48.

> ### COMMODITY PRICE INDEX
>
> Competition from America is causing problems for Australia's beef industry. Australia's exports fell 10% from 1993 to 1995. America's exports went up by 35% and will probably rise by another 8% this year, to 718,000 tonnes. Australian cattle prices have gone down by 60% since 1994. However, Australian beef exports will probably go up by 40% next year, due to rising demand in Asia.

9.2 Game

Study the grid below. Choose three spaces. Mark them with a circle but don't show your partner. Ask questions to find out which spaces your partner chose.

Example   Fall/dramatic – sales
Was there a dramatic fall in sales?
Did sales fall dramatically?

Recovery – market share
Was there a recovery in the market share this week?
Did the market share recover this week?

If you choose a wrong circle, your partner says 'No'. Take turns to ask. The winner is the first to guess all three circles.

	sales	profits	turnover	market share	share costs
fall/dramatic					
rise/steady					
increase/slight					
drop/sharp					
recovery					

9.3 Describing graphs

One person uses the information below and the other looks at the information in **File 12** on page 84.

Student A

Look at the graphs below from *The Economist*. Six titles are missing. Describe each graph to your partner and he/she will give you the missing titles. Then listen and do the same for your partner. Write in the correct title and then check your answers with your partner.

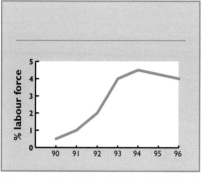
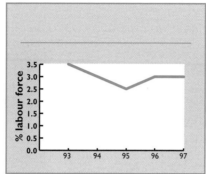
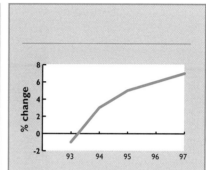

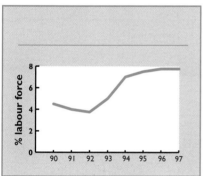
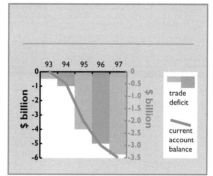
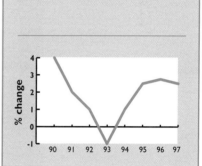

Czech Republic consumer prices
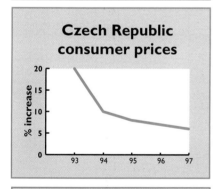

Switzerland balance of payments
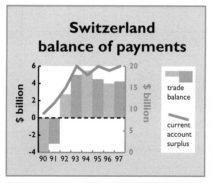

Portugal balance of payments
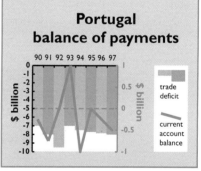

Switzerland consumer prices

Switzerland GDP
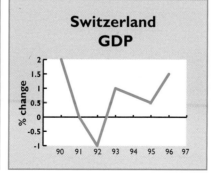

Portugal consumer prices
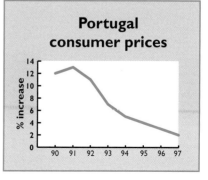

9.4 **Crossword**

One person uses the information below and the other looks at the information in **File 13** on page 85.

Student A
Complete the crossword with your partner. There are no clues but your partner has the words you need and you have the words they need. You can say anything you like to help your partner but of course, you can't say the missing word.

Example **B** *What's 14 across?*
A *The money you spend on a product or services.*

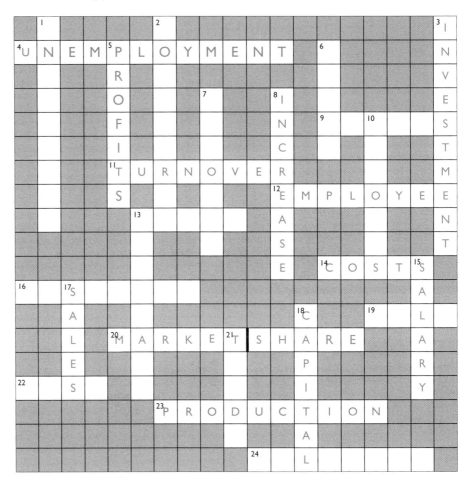

9.5 The changing economy

One person uses the information below and the other looks at the information in **File 14** on page 85.

Student A

1 Study the information in the table below. You and your partner have similar tables but some information is missing. Complete the table by asking your partner questions.

Example **A** *Did retail sales increase or decrease in Britain?*
B *They increased by 2%.*

A *Did GDP go up or down in the USA?*
B *It went up by 1.7%.*

% change between 1995 and 1996				
	GDP	Retail sales	Consumer prices	Wages
Australia	+4.8		+3.8	+2.8
Britain	+1.9		+2.1	+3.5
Canada	+0.6	+1.1	+1.5	
France	+0.9	−2.5		+1.6
Germany		−3.0	+1.4	+1.7
Italy	+0.5	−10.6		+4.8
Japan	+5.5	+1.1	+0.3	
USA		+4.9	+2.8	+3.4

2 Choose a country. Give a mini-presentation to your partner about its economic situation. Don't say its name. Your partner will try and guess which country you are talking about.

10 Company results

10.1 Away from the office

One person uses the information below and the other looks at the information in **File 15** on page 85.

Student A

You and your partner work for the same company. You are abroad for a week and you asked your partner to do some things for you whilst you are away. Phone her/him and check if there are any problems.

From:	
To:	

Close

Subject:	

Reply

Message:

Please could you see to the following while I am away –
I'll phone you next week to see how things are going.
– Make appointment with bank manager. Tuesday, if
  possible.
– Prepare sales report.
– Phone Charing Ltd. When will they pay the invoice?
– Check staff summer holidays. Arrange dates.
– Take messages; fax me anything urgent.

Forward

Print

Delete

Find out as much information as possible about each item on the list and make notes below.

Bank manager _____

Sales report _____

Invoice _____

Summer holiday dates _____

Messages _____

10.2 Financial highlights

Ericsson, a Swedish company, is the world's leading supplier in telecommunications and has over 90,000 employees in more than 130 countries.

1 Look at the two sets of figures below taken from Ericsson's annual report. Discuss with your partner the changes that have taken place in the last two years.

Example *Net sales increased by 17%, from 9,659 to 11,637.*

Ericsson
Financial Highlights 1995–1996

Table 1

	1995	1996	% change
Orders	11,017	13,771	+22%
Net sales	9,659	11,637	+17%
Pre-tax income	652	931	+30%
No. employees	84,613	89,893	+6.5%

Prices in US$ millions

Table 2

Business area	*Orders	Net sales	Profitability
Radio communications	+32%	+33%	Strong
Public telecommunications	+19%	+3%	Weak
Business networks	Satisfactory	+6%	Weak
Components	Higher	Higher	Improved

*Business area compares with the previous year

2 Now give a mini-presentation to your partner. One of you can take the first table and one of you can take the second.

3 Can you tell your partner about a company that you know in the same way?

10.3 Question game

One person uses the information below and the other looks at the information in **File 16** on page 86.

Student A
Ask your partner the following four questions, one by one. After each question, ask as many connecting questions as you can using the words in the box below. Note down how many questions you ask. Can you make more than your partner?

Example   **A** *Have you seen a good film recently?*
         B *Yes, …*
         A *Which film did you see?/Did you enjoy it?*

1 Have you seen a good film recently?
2 Have you had a problem at work recently?
3 Have you bought a present recently?
4 Have you read a good book recently?

where	when	why	what about	who
how much	how often	how many	how long	how far
do	does	did	was	were
interesting	good	expensive	comfortable	valuable

10.4 The state of the nation

1 Discuss the following topics with your partner. Speak for one minute about each topic.

Example   *Inflation has gone down recently – it is at about 3.5% – so the economy is a little better.*

Inflation in your country

Employment in your town or country

The cost of living in your town or country

The number of new companies in your local area

The construction of new buildings or roads in your area

The exchange rate for your currency

Salaries in your country

The weather in your country

2 Are there many differences between your town or your country and your partner's? Give a short summary of your discussion.

10.5 **Air travel survey**

1 Below is an air travel survey. Read the questionnaire and then take it in turns to ask the questions. Fill in the table with brief notes about you and your partner's flying habits.

		✈ AIR TRAVEL QUESTIONNAIRE	
Questions		**You**	**Your partner**
Do you often travel by air?			
Which countries have you visited?			
In the last three years how many flights have you made abroad?			
How many flights were	*for business?*		
	for pleasure?		
	for both?		
Which flight was the	*longest?*		
	the shortest?		
	the most uncomfortable?		
Have you ever	*travelled first class?*		
	missed a flight?		
	lost some luggage?		
	been delayed at an airport?		
	been highjacked?		
Do you	*enjoy flying?*		
	sleep well on a plane?		
	like the films?		
	have a favourite airline?		
	like airline food?		

2 Check that your partner's answers are correct.

Example *So, you do/don't enjoy flying, is that correct?*

3 Find five things that you both have in common and five things that are different.

10.6 **What progress have you made?**

One person uses the information below and the other looks at the information in **File 28** on page 90.

Student A

At last year's Annual General Meeting, the Chairperson of a large food retail company spoke of his/her plans for the following year.

> **Future Developments**
>
> 1 New branches in Europe
>
> 2 Petrol stations at all supermarkets
>
> 3 A new credit card for customers
>
> 4 Improved profitability
>
> 5 More staff
>
> 6 Lower prices

Have these developments happened? As a market analyst, you need to know how the company is doing. You arrange a meeting with your partner, the chairperson, and discuss each item on the list. Make notes about your conversation below.

Example   **A** *Have you opened up new branches in Europe? Where and how many?*

1

2

3

4

5

6

II Planning

II.I Future plans

Are you a pessimist or an optimist?

I Complete the chart below with your predictions for the future. You can use the ideas in the chart below or think of your own.

Topic	0–2 years	5 years	10 years
Personal life New car Move house Get married Have children			
Professional life Change company Get promotion Start your own business Move abroad			
Company Turnover and profits Expand Move office New contracts			
Your country Economy Inflation Unemployment			

2 Now tell your partner your future plans.

I think I'll …	We'll …	I'm not planning to …
I'd like to …	My company will …	I don't think I'll …
I'm planning to …	My children want to …	I want to …

11.2 Quality of life

One person uses the information below and the other looks at the information in **File 44** on page 106.

I What is important for a good quality of life? Look at the map and the information below about three towns in Spain. The information comes from a Spanish newspaper. Some information is missing. Ask your partner questions to find out what it is.

Example **A** *How many people live in Palma?*
B *320,000.*

Quality of Life

	Palma	Girona	Vitoria
POPULATION		70,576	214,234
INHABITANTS PER SQUARE KM	15,238	1,839	
GREEN (PARK) SPACE	2.5 m²		18 m²
MUNICIPAL BUDGET PER PERSON	$476	$771	
AVERAGE SPEED OF TRAFFIC KM/HR		14.4	16
KMS OF BICYCLE TRACK		12	30
PRICE OF A BUS TICKET	$1.18	$0.73	
AVERAGE TEMPERATURE	18°C		11.8°C
LEVEL OF NOISE	57 decibels	68 decibels	
COST OF HOUSING PER M²		$789	$1,187
SPORT & CULTURE		5 radio stations 2 local newspapers 1 local television channel Private sports club	3 theatres 18 cinemas Municipal sports centre

2 Did you agree with the criterion on page 54? Do you have any different ideas? What is important to you? Write your own list of criterion for a good quality of life.

1 _____

2 _____

3 _____

4 _____

5 _____

6 _____

7 _____

8 _____

9 _____

10 _____

3 Compare your list with your partner's. Do you have the same ideas? Now compare your list with the **Key 11.2**, on page 111.

4 Discussion

Does the town where you live offer a good quality of life? Discuss your town with your partner, or any other town that you like and know well.

11.3 Organizing a conference

1 You and your partner are organizing the annual international sales conference. Make a list of the factors to consider when choosing a venue. Then compare ideas with your partner.

Example *Somewhere which is easy to get to.*

1 _____

2 _____

3 _____

4 _____

5 _____

6 _____

7 _____

8 _____

9 _____

2 Compare your list with the one in **File 17** on page 86.

II.4 Choosing a conference centre

One person uses the information below and the other looks at the information in **File 35** on page 97.

Student A

1 It is your annual sales conference for 250 delegates next year. You want a conference centre in the UK or Japan. Below is an advertisement for the Holiday Inn in Manchester. Your partner has an advertisement for a hotel in Tokyo. Compare the two and make notes in the columns below.

2 Decide which hotel would be best and why. With your partner, give a mini-presentation to your boss about the hotel you have chosen.

What you need	Manchester	Tokyo
Close to airport		
Rail links		
210 single rooms		
20 double rooms		
24-hr. room service		
International cuisine		
Choice of bars		
5 meeting rooms		
I boardroom		
Secretarial and translation services		

Holiday Inn CROWNE PLAZA®

ADDRESS
Peter Street, Manchester

TEL/FAX
(0161) 236 3333
(0161) 932 4100

LOCATION
Motorway 2 km
Airport 16 km
Railway 2 km

ACCOMMODATION
303 rooms
7 suites
24-hour room service

DINING/ENTERTAINMENT
French restaurant
Cocktail bar
Buffet restaurant
Brasserie

MEETING FACILITIES
10 meeting rooms/650 people
Executive boardroom/20 people
Meeting support service
Business services
Secretarial assistance
Translation services

11.5 **Promoting a product**

1 How many ways can you promote a new product? Write a list of ideas below.

1 —————————————— 4 ——————————————

2 —————————————— 5 ——————————————

3 —————————————— 6 ——————————————

2 Compare your list with your partner and then compare your ideas with **Key 11.5** on page 111.

3 Now look at these products. How would you promote each one? Discuss your ideas with your partner.

▪ tennis rackets   ▪ brand shampoo   ▪ trainers
▪ range of health food   ▪ low-fat margarine   ▪ computer accessories

One person uses the information below and the other looks at the information in **File 19** on page 87.

Student A

4 You work for a marketing consultancy firm in Canada which specializes in advertizing through the Worldwide web (www). A client wants some advice about the best way to advertise some products in North America and the rest of the world. Give some advice about this, using the advertisement below from the Internet.

▶▶▶ HOW TO ADVERTISE YOUR PRODUCTS ◀◀◀

International press	National press	Regional press	On-line magazines	Television	Other

	Cost	Audience	Cost per 1000 consumers	Other information
Television 30-second ad	$65,000	12,000,000	$5.42	Huge audience but not targeted
National weekly magazine Full-page colour ad	$135,000	3,100,000	$43.55	Large audience, defined readership
Regional newspaper Full-page ad	$31,000	574,000	$60.31	Large local audience
www On-line magazine 1 month	$15,000	Est. 200,000	$75	Specific audience in high-income bracket

5 **Discussion**

What experience do you have of marketing? How does your company, or a company you know, promote its products or services?

11.6 Giving advice

One person uses the information below and the other looks at the information in **File 18** on page 86.

Student A

1 Look at the problems below. Imagine they are your problems. Your partner also has problems and needs help. Take it in turns to explain your problems and give advice to each other. Use some of the expressions in the box below.

- You are at work and feel terrible. You have a temperature and a headache.
- You placed an order three weeks ago and haven't received the goods yet.
- You are going to New York next month but haven't booked a flight yet.
- You have a lot of very urgent work to do but you have to meet a client in an hour.

> You'd better …
> You should …
> You'd better not …
> You shouldn't …

2 Do you have any problems that you can ask your partner for help with?

12 Comparing Information

12.1 **The working environment**

1 What makes a building a good place to work in? Can you add anything else to the list?

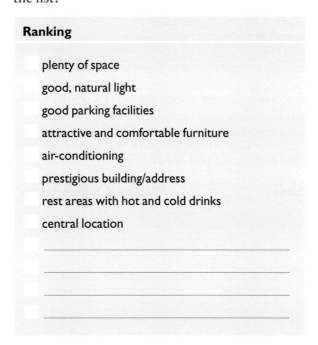

Ranking

☐ plenty of space

☐ good, natural light

☐ good parking facilities

☐ attractive and comfortable furniture

☐ air-conditioning

☐ prestigious building/address

☐ rest areas with hot and cold drinks

☐ central location

☐ _____

☐ _____

☐ _____

☐ _____

2 Rank the different factors in terms of their importance to you. Give 1 to the most important, 2 to the second most important, and so on.

3 Discuss your opinions with your partner.

> I think ...
> What do you think about ... ?
> What's the most/least important thing for you?
> ... is the most/least important because ...

4 Describe the building where you work to your partner. Mention three things you like and three things you don't like. Explain why.

12.2 New premises

One person uses the information below and the other looks at the information in **File 45** on page 107.

Student A

1 You are looking for new offices. Here are the details of what you need.

Size	500/600 m^2
Private offices	5/6 people
Open-plan office	20 people
Reception area	Medium-sized
Parking facilities	10 cars
Public transport	Near train and tube
Payment	To rent
Facilities	Air-conditioning, good lighting

2 Speak to your partner about the two locations he/she can offer and make notes in the table below.

Example A *I'm looking for some new offices for my company.*
 B *What exactly do you need?*

Features	Overlee Business Estate	Belmont House
Size		
Offices		
Reception		
Parking		
Transport		
Price		
Facilities		

3 Now discuss the information with your partner. Which is the best option? Why?

12.3 **Renting a car**

One person uses the information below and the other looks at the information in **File 20** on page 87.

Student A

1   You need to rent a car for a business trip. Your partner works for Budget Car Hire. Phone them and ask questions to get the information you need using the list below. Make notes in the table.

- One week's rental
- You want to collect and return it to the airport
- Three passengers
- A lot of space for luggage and samples of your products
- Discount price?

Class	Type of car	Price per week	Extra information

2   Now decide which car you want and make a booking.

12.4 Hiring a bike

One person uses the information below and the other looks at the information in **File 21** on page 87.

Student A

1 You work for a bike shop in Orlando, USA, where people can hire bikes, scooters, and motorbikes. Below is your price list. Your partner is a customer and phones to ask about your prices, methods of payment, insurance, and different types of bikes. You think that a motorbike is the best way to look around the city.

Orlando Bike Rentals

Tel: 234 565765

	$/day	$/24 hrs	$/week
Motorbikes			
Kawasaki Vulcan 750	$95	$155	$710
Honda Goldwing 1500	$125	$175	$875
Scooters			
Yamaha Razz	$45	$55	$225
Honda Elite	$55	$75	$320
Bicycles			
Racing bikes	$5/hr	$25	$85
Mountain bikes	$8/hr	$40	$125
Tandems	$10/hr	$50	$155

Insurance included
License necessary for motorbike rentals
No license required for scooter hire
20% Deposit
Hotel delivery and collection included

Rent a Bike! See the sights!

2 **Discussion**
- Is this a good way to go sightseeing?
- What are the advantages and disadvantages of biking?
- Have you ever hired a bike? Tell your partner about it.

12.5 The best job

1   What makes a good job? Look at the list below. Can you add anything else? Rank the points in order of importance. Then discuss your ideas with your partner. Do you agree?

Your ranking	Points	Partner's ranking
	Promotion prospects	
	Low stress level	
	High salary	
	Job security	
	Useful to the community	
	Sociable hours	
	Good holidays	
	Training possibilities	

2   What are the best jobs in your country? Discuss this with your partner and make a list below.

3   Look at the chart below. With your partner, make as many comparisons as you can from the information. How many sentences can you make?

Example   *A doctor gets the highest salary.*
   Civil engineers and pharmacists have the lowest stress levels.

The top five jobs in America

Rank	Job	$ Annual salary	Security	Social prestige	Stress level
1	Computer Analyst	42,700	Excellent	Good	Average
2	Doctor	148,000	Good	Excellent	High
3	Electrical Engineer	59,100	Excellent	Good	Average
4	Civil Engineer	55,800	Excellent	Good	Low
5	Pharmacist	47,500	Good	Good	Low

4   What are the top five jobs in your country? Is it the same or very different to America?

13 Business Travel

13.1 Airport information

1 Put the following stages in order. When you have finished, compare with your partner. Then check your answers in **Key 13.1** on page 111.

▢ Go to the boarding gate	1 Arrive at airport
▢ Go through passport control	▢ Go to arrivals terminal
▢ Check in	▢ Pass immigration control
▢ Take off	▢ Wait for flight to be called
▢ Get on plane	▢ Buy presents in duty-free shop
▢ Go through customs	▢ Wait for luggage
▢ Land	▢ Go though metal detector
▢ Taxi to hotel	

2 Now tell your partner about the last flight you took using the information above. Use the past tense.

Example *The last time I travelled by plane, I went to Germany. I arrived at the airport at about 10 o'clock, and checked in …*

13.2 Travel research

One person uses the information below and the other looks at the information in **File 22** on page 88.

Student A

1 You work for a market research firm, Consumer Choice. The French airline, Air France, wants you to do research into business travel. Ring your partner, a customer with Air France, and ask him/her some questions. Fill in the form opposite for your records.

Example **A** *Good morning, I work for a market research company, Consumer Choice. We are doing some research for Air France into business travel by air. Can I ask you a few questions?*

Name		Date	
Company		Destination	
Position		Airline	
Frequency of air travel		Next flight	
Nearest airport		Destination	
Favourite airline		Date	
Last flight		Airline	

2 Now change roles.

13.3 Crossword

One person uses the information below and the other looks at the information in **File 23** on page 88.

Student A
Complete the crossword with your partner. There are no clues but your partner has the words your need and you have the words they need. You can say anything you like to help your partner except the missing word.

Example **A** *What's 2 across?*
B *Feeling very tired after a long flight.*

13.4 Count the cost

One person uses the information below and the other looks at the information in **File 24** on page 88.

Student A

1
- ▨ You run a small computer company.
- ▨ You have to go to Amsterdam to meet some new Dutch customers.
- ▨ The details below from a local travel agent are expensive.
- ▨ Ask your partner for advice. Tell him/her about Phoenix Travel.
- ▨ Find the best prices and make some notes below.

Example   **A** *Do you know how much it costs to fly to Amsterdam? £125!!*
    B *No! There are much cheaper flights. Easy Jet do one for £70.*

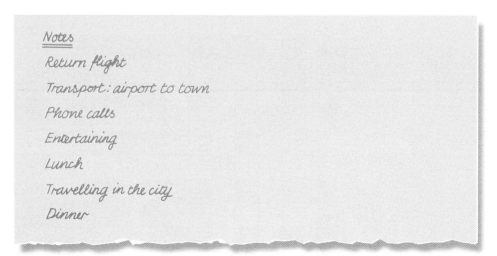

2   **Discussion**

What is the best travel offer you have ever had? And the worst? Tell your partner about it.

13.5 Eating out

1 Do you like eating in restaurants? What makes a good restaurant? Look at the following information and put them in order of importance. 1 is the most important. Do you agree with your partner?

Price	Pleasant views
High quality food	Car park available
Vegetarian menu	Convenient location
Beautiful decoration	Music in the background
Good atmosphere	Friendly service
Efficient service	Relaxed atmosphere

2 Tell your partner about a good meal you have had in a restaurant.

13.6 Healthy eating?

1 With a partner, study the list below. Decide whether each habit is a good or a bad idea when you are travelling on business.

- Coffee for breakfast
- Aeroplane food
- Drinking alcohol on flights
- Having a large lunch with wine
- Lots of fast food
- OK to carry sandwiches to eat when you get hungry
- Avoiding food you are not used to
- OK to drink coffee during meetings
- OK to eat a lot just before going to bed

2 Look at the picture below. What kind of food is everyone eating? Is it healthy or unhealthy? What kind of food do you prefer? What do you eat in your country?

14 Company Visits

14.1 Receiving a visitor

1 Work with your partner and put the conversation into the correct order. Check your answers in **Key 14.1** on page 111, then practise the conversation together.

1 Hello! Nice to see you again.
  OK. Could I leave my bags here?
  I'm fine. Did you have a good journey?
  It's very smart. When did you move in?
  Hello, how are you?
  So the business is doing well?
  Yes. Thanks for sending the driver.
  Not at all. Shall we look around the factory now?
  About 6 months ago. We needed more space.
  That's very good.
  Of course. What do you think of our new office?
  Yes. Sales have increased by 50% this year.
13 Here we are. Put this hard hat on and then we can go in.

2 Now look at the picture below. What is happening in the factory? Discuss the picture with your partner.

68

14.2 **Welcoming a visitor**

1 Your have a visitor in your office. Have a conversation using the following flow chart.

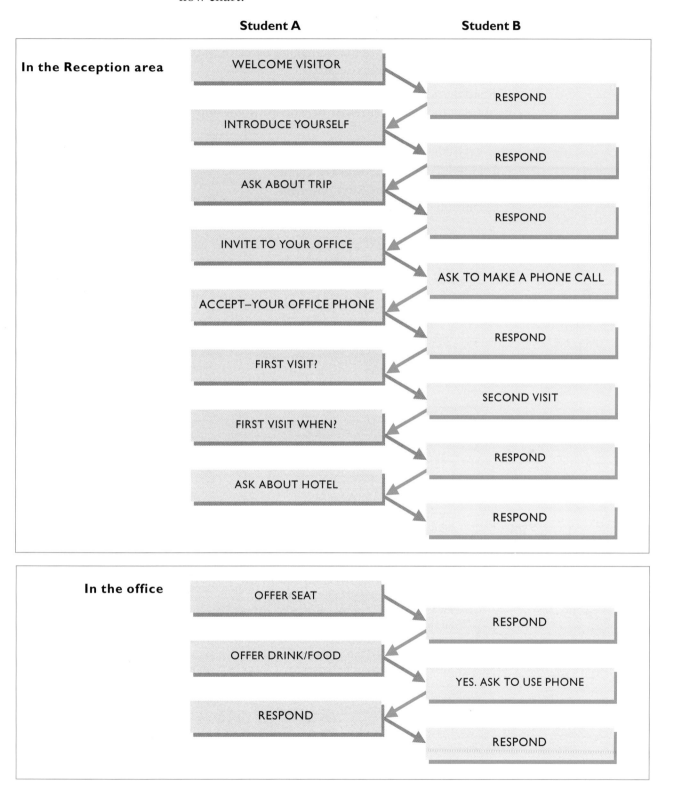

2 Now change roles and repeat the conversation.

14.3 Interview

One person uses the information below and the other looks at the information in **File 36** on page 98.

Student A

You are looking for a new job and have an interview for the post advertized below. Your partner is the Managing Director of the company and will ask you some questions about yourself.

Read the advertisement and prepare some information for the interview. Make notes in the space below. At the end ask some questions, for example, about the following:

- Salary
- Holidays
- Company car
- Pension
- Travel
- Types of client
- Anything else?

Personal details _____

Education _____

Work experience _____

Languages _____

General information (interests) _____

Financial Conference Programmer

We are a financial publishing and communications company. We have headquarters in New York and offices in London and Hong Kong.

We are looking for a European to join the London office as Conference Programmer. You will be responsible for organizing financial conferences and meetings all over the world. You will manage a support team, prepare budgets, and work with the sales force. We are looking for someone with five years' management experience. You must be a mature professional with a good knowledge of investment management. Fluent English is essential. Two other European languages are desirable.

Request an interview by contacting

Top Management Search
85 Old Bond Street
London WC2 6DX
TEL: 0171 345 2233
FAX: 0171 345 2323
E-mail: brindl@TMS.co.uk

INTERNATIONAL CONFERENCE COMPANY

14.4 **A new managing director**

One person uses the information below and the other looks at the information in **File 25** on page 89.

Student A
You work for a top telecommunications company. You are looking for a new managing director. There are two final candidates: a woman from the United States and a man from Sweden.

1 Read this article about the first candidate, Candace Johnson, and make some notes on the pad below.

Candace Johnson 'The Satellady'

'I grew up in a satellite family', says Candace Johnson. Her father ran telecommunications policy in the White House under two presidents. Johnson built her own radio when she was six.

She did not at first make a career in satellites. She first studied music. By the time she was twenty-three, she had three degrees and then became a producer at America's biggest classical music radio station. Here, she met Adrien Meisch, Luxembourg's ambassador to the USA, and married him. She then joined a small broadcasting business, and sold it a year later for several million dollars.

In 1982 Johnson went to live in Luxembourg with her husband, where she saw many opportunities in the broadcasting world. She launched the first European Television Satellite and brought multichannel television to 40% of Europe's viewers.

In 1990, Johnson started Teleport Europe, now Europe's biggest private satellite communications network. Since 1995, she has been working on a new project: Europe Online, a multilingual on-line service for over 300,000 people a day.

Name

Nationality

Education

Business background

Present business activity

Interesting facts

2 Use your notes to tell your colleague about Candace Johnson.

3 Now listen to your partner's description of the second candidate, Anders Steele, from Sweden, and make notes below.

Name

Nationality

Education

Business background

Present business activity

Interesting facts

4 Discuss and compare the two candidates. Who should get the job? Explain why.

14.5 Manufacturing biscuits

McVitie's is part of United Biscuits, Britain's biggest biscuit company. Robert McVitie had a baker's shop in Edinburgh in the 1830s. His son, also Robert, decided to concentrate on biscuits and employed Alexander Grant to help with the family business. Grant created the first Digestive biscuit and the company still uses his secret recipe. Here are some more facts about McVitie's and biscuits in general.

The number of McVitie's Digestive biscuits baked in a year could go round the world four times.

Amundsen, the first man to reach the South Pole, took some McVitie's biscuits with him on the journey in 1911.

British people eat an average of 11.4 kilos of biscuits a year!

The biscuit market in the UK is the largest in the European Union: £1.7 billion.

1 Look at the diagram below showing the production process of McVitie's Digestive biscuit. The pictures are in the wrong order. With your partner decide which order they should go in and write the correct numbers (1–9) in the boxes. Then check your answers in **Key 14.4** on page 111.

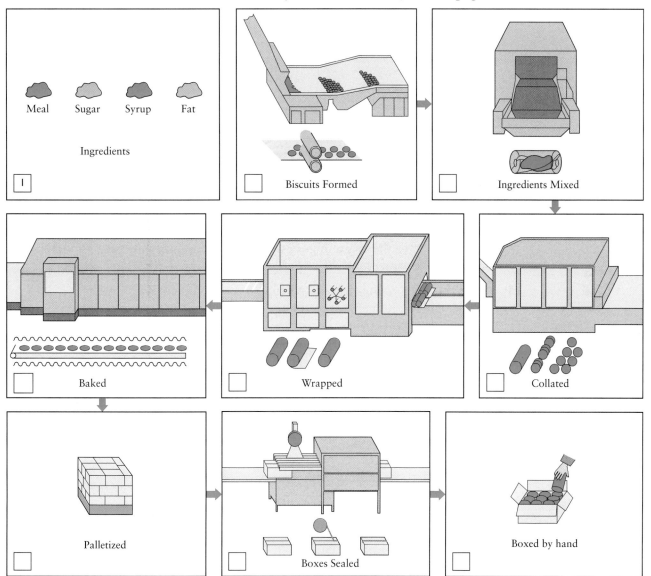

| Meal | Sugar | Syrup | Fat |

Ingredients

I

Biscuits Formed

Ingredients Mixed

Baked

Wrapped

Collated

Palletized

Boxes Sealed

Boxed by hand

Glossary
Ingredients food needed to make the biscuits
Collated collected together
Wrapped packaged
Palletized put into large crates for transport

2 Imagine that you work for McVitie's. Prepare a mini-presentation together describing the production process to some visitors. Correct each other if necessary. Who makes the least mistakes?

3 Take it in turns to describe the process in your country for each situation below.

- Renting new office space
- Applying for a passport
- Learning to drive
- Getting a place at a university

15 Tackling Problems

15.1 If I were rich …

One person uses the information below and the other looks at the information in **File 26** on page 90.

Student A
Below you have the beginnings of five sentences and the endings of another five sentences – a total of ten. Your partner has the other half of each sentence.

1 Read these beginnings to your partner and match them with his/her correct ending. Remember to change the verb into the correct form.

Example   **A** *If I were rich* …
          B … *I'd sail around the world.*

If I (to be) rich …
If I (to win) the lottery …
If I (to go) on a training course …
If I (to open) a new office …
If I (to get) a pay rise …

2 Now match these endings with your partner's beginnings.

… I (to learn) to speak good English.
… I (to get) his job.
… I (to give) it to charity.
… I (to start) my own company.
… I (to go back) to university.

15.2 Supposing ...

One person uses the information below and the other looks at the information in **File 27** on page 90.

Student A

1 Complete the following sentences in any way you like with two or three ideas. Keep your ideas in your head.

Example   A   *If I were President of my country, I'd increase taxes, spend more money on education, and introduce national service.*

- If I were president of my country …
- If I lost 10 kilos …
- If I learnt to fly …
- If my neighbours made a lot of noise at night …
- If a company offered me a good job abroad …

2 Now discuss with your partner what they would do in the same situations. Tell your partner what you would do in each situation. Do you agree?

Example   A   *Supposing you were president of your country. What would you do?*
          B   *Well, I think I'd cut taxes, cut the defence budget, and give more money to healthcare. How about you?*
          A   *I'd increase taxes, spend more money on education, and introduce National Service.*

15.3 Dream possessions

1 Think of five things that you would like to have and write them in the spaces below.

Example   *A yacht*

1 _____
2 _____
3 _____
4 _____
5 _____

2 Now explain to your partner why you would like these things. Take it in turns.

Example   *I'd like a yacht, because I'd like to sail to exotic parts of the world.*

15.4 Would you ever …?

I When would you …

… jump from a second-floor window?
… travel around the world on a bicycle?
… take a job with a lower salary than you have now?
… complain in a restaurant?
… kill someone?
… get very drunk?
… give up learning English?
… start writing poetry?
… run ten kilometres?

2 Discuss these strange situations with your partner.

Example   **A** *I'd jump from a second-floor window if there was a fire.*
          B *Yes, I agree. If there was a fire, I'd jump too.*

15.5 Choosing a candidate

You and your partner represent the European branch of a Korean electronics company. You are looking for someone to expand the sales office in Brussels. There are three candidates for the job. Look at the information below, discuss the three candidates with your partner, and then decide who is best. Before you begin, look at your different roles in the boxes **A** and **B**.

Essential	Desirable
English, French, third European language	Knowledge of Korean
Prepared to travel a lot	Experience of South Korea/Korean company
Sales experience	Experience of business in the Far East
Experience of working in Belgium	Initiative

Student A
You are impressed by qualifications. You think experience is good but you would take a risk with someone young and enthusiastic. For you a good academic background is important and knowledge beyond the specific job.

Student B
You don't like people with lots of academic qualifications. You started work at 15 and didn't go to university. But you have lots of experience, you worked hard, and succeeded in everything. For you, the most important things are experience, knowledge of the job, and the ability to work hard.

JANINE PASCALE

Belgian, 32

Fluent French, Spanish, German

Started work at 16 in Sales Department of small electronics company

Now a sales manager, Anglo-Korean marketing company

MBA at night-school in Paris

Intelligent, quick to learn, hard-working ambitious

Wants to live in Brussels

Underpaid in present post and wants a higher salary

NORBERT BENOIT

French, 38, speaks a little English

No university education, started work at 18

8 years as Assistant Manager of an electronics firm in Grenoble

Little experience of marketing

Wants a challenge and something new

Earns a good salary in present post

MICHELE LING

French, 24

MBA – top of the class

No work experience – just graduated

Holiday jobs with marketing firm

Excellent ideas for the Brussels office

Intelligent, keen, hard-working

Fluent English and French

Make notes about the candidates below. You must decide on one person and explain your decision.

JANINE PASCALE

_____

_____

_____

MICHELE LING

_____

_____

_____

NORBERT BENOIT

_____

_____

_____

15.6 **Negotiating a deal**

One person uses the information below and the other looks at the information in **File 37** on page 99.

Student A

You are the IT co-ordinator for a car-hire company, Eurodrive. You want to place an order for 120 new computers for the company. Your partner works for Flexible Software Ltd. He/she has offered you a discount on the computers but you must get the best deal you can. Your boss has looked at the offer and made a few notes below. Discuss the sale with your partner, and come to an arrangement.

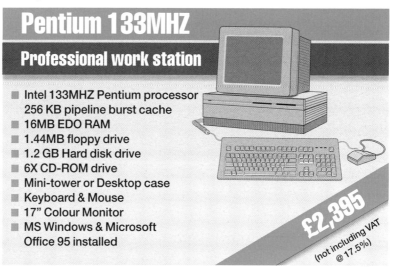

Pentium 133MHZ

Professional work station

- Intel 133MHZ Pentium processor 256 KB pipeline burst cache
- 16MB EDO RAM
- 1.44MB floppy drive
- 1.2 GB Hard disk drive
- 6X CD-ROM drive
- Mini-tower or Desktop case
- Keyboard & Mouse
- 17" Colour Monitor
- MS Windows & Microsoft Office 95 installed

£2,395
(not including VAT @ 17.5%)

> If we agree to …
> I'd like a discount of …
> Could you deliver …?
> How much …?
> That's a bit high.
> Would you agree to …?

Conditions

1 Terms of payment:

  30 days/Cash on delivery: 3% discount

2 Delivery period: 3 weeks

3 Discounts: 26 to 50 units: 3.5%

            51 units or more: 5%

4 Guarantee: One year on-site parts & labour warranty

NEW COMPUTERS

This is a good offer. But it is also a big order. Try to get a better deal:

1. Ask for 60 days.

2. Not important.

3. Ask for 10% on 100 units or over.

4. Other companies offer 2 years warranty.

Information files

File I
SEE PAGE 11

Student B

1 You are a reporter for a business magazine. You want to interview Marc Taylor for an article entitled 'My Business Day'. He is head of the UK operations of 7 Eleven, a food retailer. He is responsible for eight hundred employees in fifty-five shops.

Ask about his working day from when he gets up to when he goes to bed. Use the ideas below.

Example
What time do you get up?

- Get up?
- Arrive at the office?
- First job of the day?
- Morning activities?
- Lunch?
- Leave the office?
- Finish work?
- Physical exercise?
- Arrive home?
- Evenings?
- Bed?

2 Now interview each other in the same way about your daily routines.

File 2
SEE PAGE 12

Student B

1 Listen to your partner. He/she will read out some groups of letters very quickly and only once. Listen carefully and mark them off in the grid below.

Bingo

AEI	JYG	IYG	UWV	AGE	VGE
IEA	GYJ	EIG	VWU	AJI	VJE
EAI	YGJ	IEG	WUV	JAE	UJI
GJG	PTY	FAE	HEL	IRT	OWQ
WOW	SQU	TAU	ROT	QZC	FHR
ROE	BRU	LKJ	SPR	POA	NEG

2 Now you read out the list of letters below to your partner who will mark them off on their grid.

VNM	TRE	PEU	TSE	TWP
GAE	ERT	PCT	FJI	OUI
JAE	BUE	WPT	UIJ	

Now compare your grid with the one in **Key 2.1** on page 109.

File 3

SEE PAGE 14

Student B

1 You are the Receptionist in two different top-class hotels in Seoul, South Korea (Imagine that you are a different person each time). Your partner is visiting the city on business and needs somewhere to stay. He/she rings both hotels for information. Answer your partner's questions using the table below. Your partner will choose a hotel.

2 When he/she rings back, take the booking.

Seoul Plaza Hotel

SUPRANATIONAL
— H O T E L S —

Location: Downtown Seoul near banks, embassies, government offices, and shopping centres

Airport: 8 km Kimp'o International

Railway: 2 km

Rooms: 479

Business services: Translation, secretarial, fax

Conference facilities: Yes

Restaurants and bars: International

Prices: Singles from $255
Doubles from $315

Misc. Currency US$

SEOUL INTERNATIONAL HOTEL

Location: *10km west of city centre*

Airport: *28km Kimp'o International*

Transport: *Free shuttle service to city centre. Close to subway*

Rooms: *623 from $150*

Restaurants: *9: Korean, Japanese, Chinese, Indian*

Lounge/bars: *4*

Recreation: *Golf, tennis, swimming, health club, casino, and water sports on the Han-gang River.*

Dinner/theatre: *Traditional Korean dance*

Convention centre: *Translation in 6 languages, secretarial services*

File 4

SEE PAGE 15

Student B

1 You work for Effective Business Events, a corporate entertainment company, in Oxford. A client phones you for information about some advertisements in the local paper. You have the details in front of you: the costs, the discounts, the times, and so on. Answer your client's questions and make the necessary arrangements.

The Oxford Playhouse

Jaleo Flamenco
Good for non-native English speakers – a dance
15% reduction for 6 or more
Snack bar; restaurant
Good restaurants nearby

Balloon Flights

Insurance included
Maximum 5 people
£70 per person
1 hour flight

Salsa Ache Havana Latin Disco

Starts 8 p.m.
Bar meals

The Talkhouse at Stanton-St-John

Eat as much as you want
Traditional English food
Evening meals £2 extra a head

2 Discussion

What do you like doing in the evenings? Tell your partner three things that you like doing and three things that you don't like doing. Would you go out together one evening?

File 5
SEE PAGE 17

Student B

1 Your partner will give you some details about a company. Listen and complete the first box with information about the company.

2 Now complete the spaces in the second box with information about any company. You can invent a company. Read your description to your partner as quickly as possible. He/she will check the information by asking questions as you read.

Example
I'm sorry, what did you say?
I'm sorry, what do they produce?

Your partner's company

_____ is a company based in _____ in _____ . The company employs about _____ workers. They produce/provide _____ for the _____ industry. Their main market is _____ and they export to _____ . The turnover is about _____ .

Your company

_____ is a company based in _____ in _____ . The company employs about _____ workers. They produce/provide _____ for the _____ industry. Their main market is _____ and they export to _____ . The turnover is about _____ .

File 6
SEE PAGE 21

Student B

You receive a phone call from someone who wants to sell you a product. You are interested in it and would like to have a demonstration in your office. Ask a few questions about the product (special features, size, weight, price, and so on). Arrange a day and a time for a demonstration.

File 7
SEE PAGE 25

Student B

You are leaving the Central Hotel, New York, and want to pay the bill.

- Your assistant reserved a single room a week before you arrived.
- When you arrived only a double room was available.
- You think the hotel should charge for a single room.
- The invoice is for all your expenses.
- You paid the mini-bar and laundry bills separately.
- Speak to the Manager and make a complaint.

File 8
SEE PAGE 33

Student B

Compare your ideas with the list below. Tick the ideas you agree with, and add any of your own which are not included.

- prepare an agenda in advance
- provide a big table
- provide comfortable seating
- make sure there are no interruptions
- have a time limit for the meeting
- have a different chairperson at each meeting
- provide drinks and refreshments
- give advanced warning for the meeting
- agree on the purpose of the meeting. For example, giving information, problem solving
- take minutes and write a report after the meeting
- make an action plan for each issue

Now each choose the **five** most important things. Compare with your partner. Do you agree?

File 9

SEE PAGE 38

Your partner is your boss, a director. You are a Personal Assistant in charge of his/her diary below. There are many changes for next week's appointments. In the diary, the blue writing shows the changes. Your notes below give more details about the changes for each day. Explain the new arrangements to your boss and answer any questions.

DAY	AM	PM
MONDAY	Production meeting 09.00 Report	17.15 Golf match, Tony
TUESDAY	13.30 lunch, Brown's	Squash cancelled
WEDNESDAY	08.00-13.00 Safety Inspection	
THURSDAY	London: 07.35 train to London; return 16.45	
FRIDAY	09.30 Board Meeting 2 people for lunch: Hilton	19.30 Theatre

Your notes

MONDAY:	the production manager will finish the report by Friday.
WEDNESDAY:	three people from Head Office are coming: Mr Brown, Ms Davies, Mr Jackson.
FRIDAY:	the Finance Director is giving the presentation to the board.
FRIDAY:	will telephone Thurs am, to confirm how many directors for lunch.
FRIDAY:	tickets are sold out. Dinner instead? Confirm by Wednesday.

File 10

SEE PAGE 42

This is the latest programme for your partner's trip to the USA next month. Discuss the programme with your partner and check he/she has the correct details. You have made a reservation at the Heathrow Hilton for the last day, because the flight is late. Ask if she/he wants to stay at the hotel or go straight home.

NEW YORK AND BOSTON TRIP Programme

Day One 15th

Flight TWA 234   London-New York
Dep. 12.35   Arr. 19.00

AXIS car at airport,
meet driver at Information Desk

Highbury Inn 3 nights

20.30	Dinner with Mr Chandler, Export Manager, Mrs Lawson, Senior Analyst

Day Two 16th

09.00	AXIS car at hotel visit AXIS office
09.45	Meet Mrs Lawson to discuss new software application
12.45	Lunch Mrs Lawson
14.15	Meeting Mr Chandler
15.00-17.30	Visit software development office
19.30	Opera, meet at hotel at 18.30

Day Three 17th

Morning free

11.00	Axis car hotel, visit office
12.15	Buffet lunch
13.00-18.00	Seminar 'Integrated Solutions'
20.00	Dinner with seminar participants

Day Four 18th

07.45   Taxi to airport

Flight United Airlines UA 181 New York to Boston
Dep. 09.45   Arr. 11.35

```
Boston Park Hotel 3 nights

Visit Boston Software 2000 fair

Boston Showplace Centre

Appointments
15.00   David Berkley Mansoft        Stand 012-B
16.00   Alice Seymour Delware        Stand 343-B
17.00   Peter Aliss KPA              Stand 310-B
16.30   Mary Evans MCG               Stand 213-A


Day Five 19th
---------------------------------------------

Appointments
09.30   Helen Burns, Stock solutions Stand 122-A

11.30   Mr Archer, St Soft           Stand 187-A

16.00   George Clarke, Studio 67     Stand 165-B


Day Six 20th
---------------------------------------------

Visit fair


Day Seven 21st
---------------------------------------------

Flight DE 141 Boston - New York - London
Dep. 08.35        Arr. 21.40

Heathrow Hilton Hotel


Day Eight 22nd
---------------------------------------------

08.30           Company car at hotel
                return home
```

File 11

SEE PAGE 43

Student B

1 Answer your partner's questions using the information below.

COMMODITY PRICE INDEX

Nickel prices fell below $7,000 a tonne on the London Metal Exchange last week. Last year demand for nickel went up by 12% to 881,000 tonnes. This was due to an increase in the production of steel. In 1994 there was a rise of 16%.

MEDICAL COSTS

The cost of healthcare is increasing in the West. In OECD countries, spending on medical goods was just under 8% of GDP in 1994. This was about the same as in 1993. America is the biggest spender. It spent 14.3% of its GDP on healthcare in 1994. This is more than $3,500 per person.

2 Now look at the following statistics. Complete the spaces with the figures in the boxes. Then check with your partner for the correct figures.

Example
A *Can I check some information with you? The average Norwegian spent $67 on music last year. Is that right?*
B *Yes, that's correct.*

MUSIC SALES

Norway spends the most on music. Last year, Norwegians spent US$67 a head on compact discs, records, and cassettes. From _____ to _____ sales in Norway rose by _____. Sales in Japan rose by _____ to _____ per person. America's music industry is the biggest, but sales per person are _____.

147%   148% $67   1995 $61 $48   1990

COMMODITY PRICE INDEX

Competition from America is causing problems for Australia's beef industry. Australia's exports fell _____ from _____ to 1995. America's exports went up by _____ and will probably rise by another _____ this year, to _____ tonnes. Australian cattle prices have gone down by _____ since _____. However, Australian beef exports will probably go up by 40% next year, due to rising demand in Asia.

1994   10%   718,000   8%   60%   1993   35%

File 12

SEE PAGE 45

Student B

Look at the graphs below from *The Economist*. Six titles are missing. Describe each graph to your partner and he/she will give you the missing titles. Then listen and do the same for your partner. Write in the correct title and then check your answers with your partner.

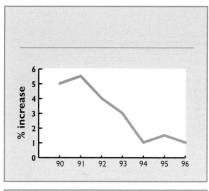

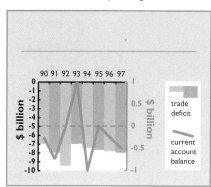

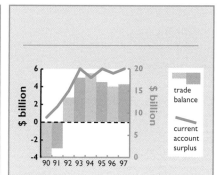

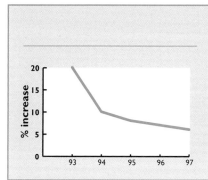

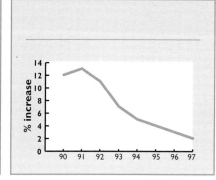

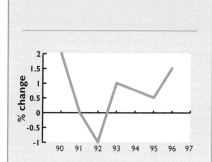

Czech Republic GDP

Czech Republic balance of payments

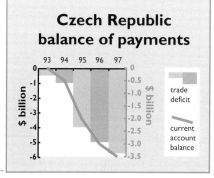

Switzerland unemployment

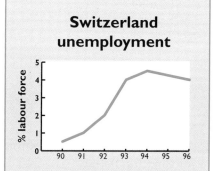

Portugal GDP

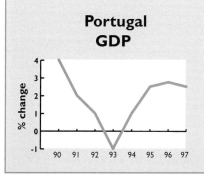

Czech Republic unemployment

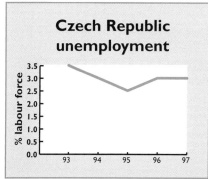

Portugal unemployment

File 13
SEE PAGE 46

Student B
Complete the crossword with your partner. There are no clues but your partner has the words you need and you have the words they need. You can say anything you like but you can't say the missing word.

Example
A *What's 19 across?*
B *Another word for decrease.*

[Crossword grid with answers:]
INFLATION, WORKFORCE, EXPORTS, GRAPH, PRICES, IMPORTS, DEBTS, RESEARCH, DECREASE, FALL, TRADE, RISE, DELIVERY

File 14
SEE PAGE 47

Student B
1 Study the information in the following table. You and your partner have similar tables but some information is missing. Complete the table by asking your partner questions.

Example
B *Did wages go up in Australia?*
A *Yes, by 2.8%.*

B *What happened to retail sales in Japan?*
A *They increased by 19%.*

% change between 1995 and 1996

	GDP	Retail Sales	Consumer prices	Wages
Australia		+5.4	+3.8	
Britain	+1.9	+2.0	+2.1	+3.5
Canada		+1.1	+1.5	+1.9
France	+0.9	−2.5	+2.2	
Germany	−0.3	−3.0	+1.4	+1.7
Italy	+0.5		+3.9	+4.8
Japan	+5.5			+2.3
USA	+1.7	+4.9		+3.4

2 Choose a country from the chart above. Give a mini-presentation to your partner about its economic situation. Don't say its name. Your partner will try and guess which country you are talking about.

File 15
SEE PAGE 48

Student B
You and your partner work for the same company. Your partner is away but sent you the e-mail below with a list of things to do. When your partner phones, report on the progress you have made. Use your notes on the next page.

From:
To:
Subject:
Message:
Please could you see to the following while I am away –
I'll phone you next week to see how things are going.
– Make appointment with bank manager. Tuesday, if possible.
– Prepare sales report.
– Phone Charing Ltd. When will they pay the invoice?
– Check staff summer holidays. Arrange dates.
– Take messages; fax me anything urgent.

Close · Reply · Forward · Print · Delete

Bank manager:	On holiday for 2 weeks.
Sales report:	Where are figures for Japan and Malaysia?
Invoice:	Will pay next month.
Holidays:	Will check dates
Messages:	Phone Sales office in Turkey. Urgent.
	New assistant is ill. Will start next week.
	Apologies from Charing Ltd. re. unpaid invoice.

File 17 SEE PAGE 55

Student B
Compare your ideas with the list below. Tick the ideas you agree with.

- Good location
- Type of meeting rooms available
- Comfortable accommodation
- Good quality food
- Leisure facilities
- Business facilities
- Conference facilities
- Good prices and discounts

File 16 SEE PAGE 50

Student B
Ask your partner the following four questions, one by one. Then, after each question, ask as many connecting questions as you can using the words in the box below. Note down how many questions you ask. Can you make more than your partner?

Example
B *Have you been to a conference recently?*
A *Yes, I …*
B *Where was the conference?/Was it useful?/Who was there?*

1 Have you been to a conference recently?

2 Have you had a good holiday recently?

3 Have you bought a present recently?

4 Have you travelled by air recently?

where	how much	do	interesting
when	how often	does	good
why	how many	did	expensive
what about	how long	was	comfortable
who	how far	were	valuable

File 18 SEE PAGE 58

Student B
1 Look at the four problems below. Imagine they are your problems. Your partner also has some problems and needs some help. Take it in turns to explain your problems and give advice to each other. Use some of the language in the box below.

- You forgot that you were meeting a client at the airport at 9 o'clock. It is now 8.50. It takes 30 minutes to get to the airport.
- You have to send an important document to a customer by 6 p.m. It is now 5.20 in the rush hour and the customer's office is on the other side of town.
- You find it difficult to remember new vocabulary in English.
- You are suffering from stress because of the amount of work you have.

> You'd better …
> You should …
> You'd better not …
> You shouldn't …

2 Do you have any real problems that you can ask your partner for help with?

File 19 SEE PAGE 57

Student B

4 You are the Sales Manager for a company based in Canada – you may invent a company if you wish. You want to promote your products in the best way possible. Ring your partner, a marketing consultant, and ask for some advice. Below is a list of possible products that you can sell, but choose your own if you wish.

- children's clothes
- walking boots
- ecological washing powder
- package holidays
- jewellery
- toothpaste
- CD player

5 Discussion

What experience do you have of marketing? How does your company, or a company you know, promote its products or services?

File 20 SEE PAGE 61

Student B

You work for Budget Care Hire, a car hire firm. A customer phones to ask about your prices and details. Below is a price list with car details. Answer the customers' questions and then fill out the rental form with their details.

Budget Car Hire

Class	Type of car	Price per week	Information
A	Nissan Micra	£154	4 seats, 3 doors
B	Peugeot 306	£187	5 seats, 3 doors
C	Peugeot 406	£238	5 seats, 4 doors
D	Opel Omega	£434	5 seats, 4 doors
E	Toyota Previa	£525	8 seats, automatic

Rental form Budget Car Hire

Name

Address

Date of birth ☐☐☐☐☐☐

Date licence issued ☐☐☐☐☐☐

Method of payment

Credit card

☐☐☐☐☐☐☐☐☐☐☐☐☐☐☐☐

Cheque ☐

File 21 SEE PAGE 62

Student B

1 You are in Orlando, USA, and want to do some sightseeing by bike. Your partner works in a bike shop. Phone and ask about prices, methods of payment, insurance, and types of bike. Below is a list of different types of bike, but no details. Decide which bike you would like and book it.

Motorcycles
Kawasaki Vulcan 750
Honda Goldwing 1500

Scooters
Yamaha Razz
Honda Elite

Bicycles
Racing bikes
Mountain bikes
Tandems

2 Discussion

- Is this a good way to go sightseeing?
- What are the advantages and disadvantages of biking?
- Have you ever hired a bike? Tell your partner about it.

File 22

SEE PAGE 64

Student B

1 You are a sales manager and you make regular trips to Europe, America, and Asia. Your partner works for a market research company. He/she will ring you and ask you questions about your business trips abroad. Imagine that you go abroad a lot and use many different airlines. Your partner will begin.

2 Now change roles.

You work for a market research firm, Consumer Choice. The French airline, Air France, wants you to do research into business travellers. Ring your partner, a customer with Air France, and ask him/her some questions. Fill in the form below for your records.

Example
A *Good morning, I work for a market research company, Consumer Choice. We are doing some research for Air France into business travel by air. Can I ask you a few questions?*

Name

Company

Position

Frequency of air travel

Nearest airport

Favourite airline

Last flight

Date

Destination

Airline

Next flight

Destination

Date

Airline

File 23

SEE PAGE 65

Student B
Complete the crossword with your partner. There are no clues but your partner has the words you need and you have the words they need. You can say anything you like to help your partner but of course, you can't say the missing word.

Example
A *What's 1 down?*
B *It's a person who goes on a plane.*

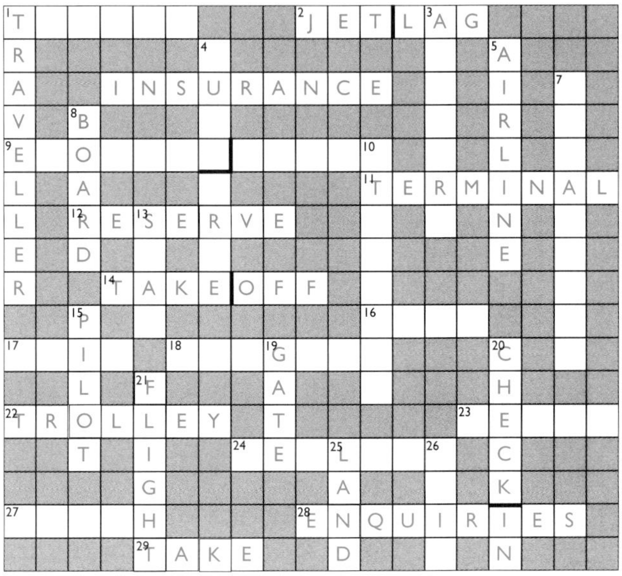

Crossword (partially completed):
- 2 across: JETLAG — 3: AG
- 1 down: TRAVELLER
- INSURANCE
- 5: A; 8: B(OA...); 9: E
- 11: TERMINAL
- 12: RESERVE
- 14: TAKEOFF
- 15: P; 22: TROLLEY
- 28: ENQUIRIES
- 29: TAKE

File 24

SEE PAGE 66

Student B
1
- You run a small computer company.
- Your partner is going to Amsterdam on business.
- Your partner needs to keep his/her costs low.
- You know Amsterdam quite well and have some details below about cheap deals.
- Answer your partner's questions using the information below.

Example
A *Do you know how much it costs to fly to Amsterdam? £125!!*
B *No! There are much cheaper flights. Easy Jet do one for £70.*

£££££££££££££££££££££££££££££££££££££
BARGAIN PRICES TO AMSTERDAM!
£££££££££££££££££££££££££££££££££££££

Easy Jet flight	£70
Train to city	£10
Taxi to city	£20
Phone card	£2
Entertaining Café Americain tea/coffee	£4
Lunch Sandwiches Café Americain	£4
Riverboat day bus Go everywhere by canal	£9
Dinner at airport	£4

PHONE 0181 630 1111 FOR DETAILS

2 Discussion

What is the best travel offer you have ever had? And the worst?

Tell your partner about it.

File 25

SEE PAGE 71

Student B

You work for a top telecommunications company. You are looking for a new Managing Director. There are two final candidates: a woman from the United States and a man from Sweden.

I Read the article about the second candidate, Anders Steele, a businessman from Sweden, and make some notes on the pad below.

> Name
> Nationality
> Education
> Business background
> Present business activity
> Interesting facts

Young man with new ideas

Anders Steele began working when he was twelve years old. He repaired radios, televisions and video recorders for his friends and family. He went to school during the day and worked every evening in his father's garage.

In 1984, he graduated with a degree in Telecommunications Engineering from Frankfurt University. He then went to America to study English for two months but stayed two years to do a Master's Degree in Business Administration.

He returned home and borrowed $25,000 from family and friends to set up a small company producing parabolic antennas for satellite television. It is a huge success. The company now employs fifty people and has a turnover of $2.5 million.

Steele would like to become the Managing Director of a large telecommunications company but his real ambition is to open a chain of video-conferencing centres all over Europe: 'video-conferencing is the future', he says.

2 Then listen to your partner's description of Candace Johnson, the first candidate. Make some notes below.

> Name
> Nationality
> Education
> Business background
> Present business activity
> Interesting facts

3 Now use your notes about Anders Steele to present him to your partner.

4 Discuss and compare the two candidates. Who should get the job? Explain why.

File 26 SEE PAGE 74

Student B
Below you have the beginnings of five sentences and the endings of another five sentences - a total of ten. Your partner has the other half of each sentence.

I Listen to your partner read out some sentence beginnings. Match them with your endings below. Remember to change the verb into the correct form.

Example
A *If I were rich* …
B … *I'd sail* around the world.

… I (to sail) around the world.
… I (to take out) a mortgage.
… I (to invest) it in shares.
… I (to know) how the computer system works.
… They (to need) more staff.

2 Now read these sentence beginnings to your partner and match them with the correct ending.

If I (to make) lots of money …
If I (to have) enough capital …
If I (to lose) my job …
If I (to go) to England …
If my boss (to resign) …

File 27 SEE PAGE 75

Student B
I Complete the following sentences in any way you like with two or three ideas. Keep you ideas in your head.

Example
B *If I spoke perfect English, I'd look for a better job and perhaps work in America.*

▪ If I spoke perfect English …
▪ If I saw an unidentified flying object (UFO) …
▪ If I lost all my money and my passport abroad …
▪ If I found a valuable object in the street …
▪ If I crashed a friend's car …

2 Discuss with your partner what they would do in the same situations. Tell your partner what you would do in each situation. Do you agree?

Example
A *Supposing you spoke perfect English. What would you do?*
B *Well, I think I'd do some translation work for the British embassy or teach English to local business people. What would you do?*
A *I'd look for a better job and perhaps work in America.*

File 28 SEE PAGE 52

You are the Chairperson on the board of a large food retail company. At last year's Annual General Meeting, you spoke of your plans for the following year. Your partner is a market analyst and wants to know what has happened since the AGM. Look at the information below and answer your partner's questions.

Future Developments
I New branches in Europe
2 Petrol stations at all supermarkets
3 A new credit card for customers
4 Improved profitability
5 More staff
6 Lower prices

Area	Last year	This year	Notes
Number of branches	215	227	Total: 12, UK: 2, France: 3, Italy: 3, Poland: 4
Petrol stations	0	15	Hypermarkets only
New credit card	No	No	Planed for next year
Profits after tax	£160m	£190m	19%
Staff	8,600	9,718	+13% needed for new stores
Prices		+2%	Inflation at 4.5%

File 29

SEE PAGE 9

Student B

1 You are attending a trade conference with your partner. You have a fax with the names of other delegates and some basic information about each person. Some of it is difficult to read. Your partner has the missing information. Ask questions to find the missing information.

Who ...	... is from ... ?
	... works for ... ?
	... works in ... ?

What nationality is ... ?
Where does ... work?
Who does ... work for?

FAX

To

From

Ref International Trade Conference

Name	From	Company	Based in	Position
	Chile		Santiago	Sales Manager
Reiner Mattner		Siemens		Regional Sales Director
Watanabe	Japan	Mitsubushi	Tokyo	
	South Korea	Daewoo		Finance Director
Angelos Angelidis	Indonesia		Jakarta	
Jacinto Sileci		Petrobrás		General Manager

2 You are now at the conference. In pairs, each take the role of one of the people in the fax above. Imagine you are meeting for the first time and act out the conversation with your partner.

Example   **A**   *Hello, I'm* ————————— .

B   *How do you do? I'm* ————————— .

I work for ————————— . *And you?*

A   *I* ————————— .

91

File 30

SEE PAGE 10

Student B

1 Find out from your partner the missing information about the managers and divisions of TLM PLC.

> Who is the ...?
> Who is responsible for ...?
> Who is in charge of ...?
> What does ... do?
> Who is ... in charge of?

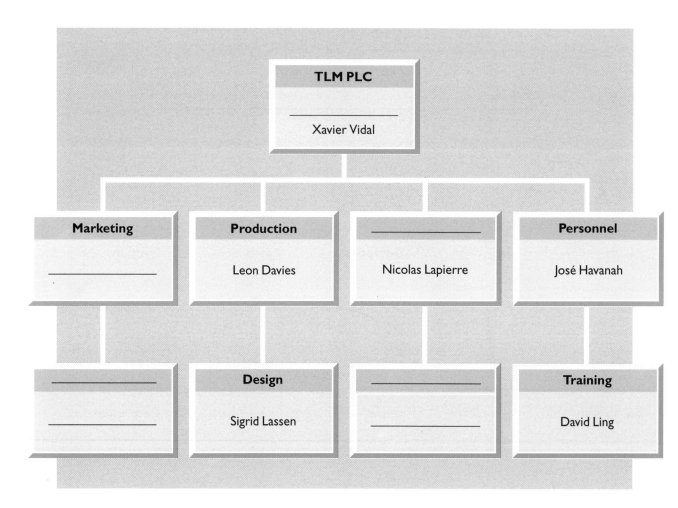

2 Now use the same questions to ask your partner about their company or an imagined one. Use the information to draw an organization chart of the company they describe.

File 31

SEE PAGE 19

Student B

1 You work for Office World, a company selling office furniture. Your partner wants to equip a new office. Answer their questions. Use the following page from your catalogue. Give details about dimensions, prices, and colour.

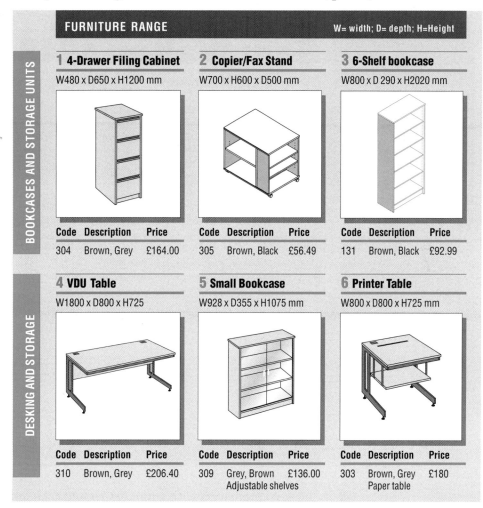

2 Complete the form below with the details of your customer's order.

File 32

SEE PAGE 22

Student B

1 Read the story about Sam Walton, the world's richest self-made man. Some information is missing. Complete the text by asking your partner questions using the words in the box below.

Sam Walton 1918–1992
A story of American free enterprise

The American entrepreneur, Sam Walton, died in 1992. He had a chain of 1,752 stores across America. His company was worth $1.6 billion.

Walton was born in 1918 and studied __9__ at university. To pay for his studies, he worked as a waiter. Then he borrowed $25,000 and bought a franchise store: the Ben Franklin 'Five and Dime'. When Walton arrived, the store was losing money but soon made a profit with his new ideas.

Walton wanted to start up discount stores across small town America, but the Ben Franklin company disagreed.

So, with __10__ he opened the first Wal-Mart Discount Store in __11__ in 1962. Customers could buy anything from jeans to bread.

Walton succeeded because __12__ and because he knew how to make money. For example, he learnt __13__ and could visit five or six stores across the USA in a day.

Walton soon built a network of over __14__ stores, based in rural parts of the country. He used __15__ to supply the stores with fresh produce and had a satellite linked to store computers.

Walton died of Leukaemia at the age of __16__ . Today, the Walton family still control Wal-Mart stores. The company has a reputation for friendly service, low prices, and profit-sharing. Wal-Mart's food labels are still called 'Sam's American Choice'.

9 _____

10 _____

11 _____

12 _____

13 _____

14 _____

15 _____

16 _____

What	Who	Where	Why
What	How many	How	How

2 Check your answers with your partner and then look at **Key 5.1** on page 110, and check you asked the right questions.

3 **Discussion**

Do you know any interesting stories from your country about successful rich entrepreneurs and self-made business people? If you do, tell your partner the story.

File 33

SEE PAGE 36

Student B

Your company, Microtex, produces micro-switches and employs 60 staff. The market is changing rapidly, and the company is introducing expensive technology. To survive, Microtex must make some savings and reduce costs.

You have a meeting with a colleague to discuss the options. Look at the information below. Present the two ideas to your partner. Your partner will then present two more ideas to you. Makes notes below. Then decide together which is the best solution.

Remember to consider the following:

- how much money each idea will save
- how each idea will affect productivity
- how to avoid problems with the unions

You must find a solution. If not, the company will go out of business!

Solution	Costs	Savings	Advantages	Disadvantages
4-day working week and 20% reduction in pay	None, but problems with the unions could be expensive, strikes	£120,000 a year	Reduce level of production to meet market needs	Opposition from unions, strikes
10 workers over 60 years old take early retirement	£450,000 compensation for early retirement	£150,000 a year	Some of these workers have low levels of productivity and high salaries	In 5 years, these workers will retire at no extra cost

File 34

SEE PAGE 37

Student B

You want a two-hour meeting with your partner and two other people, Mr Harris and Ms Wilson. The meeting is for next Monday or Tuesday. Speak to your partner and find a time for the meeting. Complete the information on the diary page below.

Your office hours are 9am to 1.30pm and 2.30 to 5.30pm. When can you have the meeting?

Diary	You	Mr Harris	Ms Wilson	Your partner
Monday am			Attend training session all morning	
Monday pm		2.30 Susan Willis 3.30 Committee meeting all afternoon		
Tuesday am			Job interviews approx. 2 hours	
Tuesday pm	1.30 lunch with Managing Director 3-6 Board meeting	2.30-5 Dentist	Personnel Dept meeting all afternoon	

Check your answer in **Key 8.1** on page 111 when you have finished.

File 35

SEE PAGE 56

Student B

1 It is your annual sales conference for 250 delegates next year. You are looking for a conference centre in the UK or in Japan. Look at the advertisement below for a large hotel in Tokyo. Your partner has an advertisement for a hotel in England. Compare information about the two places and make notes in the two columns below.

2 Decide which hotel is best and why. With your partner, give a mini-presentation to your boss about the hotel you choose.

Le Pacific
MERIDIEN
TOKYO

ADDRESS
– Tokyo, Japan
TEL/FAX
– (03) 3445 6711 (03) 3445 5733
GENERAL INFORMATION
– 15 minutes city centre
– 60 minutes Narita International airport
ACCOMMODATION
– 297 singles
– 144 doubles
– 41 suites
– From 21,000 yen
GUEST ROOM FACILITIES
– Cable TV, 2 phone connections, air-conditioning

RESTAURANTS AND BARS
– 6 Continental, Japanese, and Chinese cuisine
– 4 bars
SPORTS
– Swimming pool
MEETING FACILITIES
– 15 rooms, top-quality equipment
– VIP board room
– Business centre with secretarial and translation services
GENERAL
– Car rental, travel agent, shopping arcade

What you need	Manchester	Tokyo
Close to airport		
Rail links		
210 single rooms		
20 doubles		
24-hr. room service		
International cuisine		
Choice of bars		
5 meeting rooms		
1 boardroom		
Secretarial and translation services		

97

File 36

SEE PAGE 70

Student B

You are the Director of an international conference company. You are looking for a new Conference Programmer and placed the advertisement below in the national press. Today you are interviewing one candidate.

Read the advertisement and then prepare some questions for the candidate about the topics in the table on the left.

Personal details

Education

Work experience

Languages

General

information

(interests)

Financial Conference Programmer

We are a financial publishing and communications company. We have headquarters in New York and offices in London and Hong Kong.

We are looking for a European to join the London office as Conference Programmer. You will be responsible for organizing financial conferences and meetings all over the world. You will manage a support team, prepare budgets, and work with the sales force. We are looking for someone with five years' management experience. You must be a mature professional with a good knowledge of investment management. Fluent English is essential. Two other European languages are desirable.

Request an interview by contacting

Top Management Search
85 Old Bond Street
London WC2 6DX
TEL: 0171 345 2233
FAX: 0171 345 2323
E-mail: brindl@TMS.co.uk

I C C

INTERNATIONAL CONFERENCE COMPANY

The candiate may ask further questions about salary, holidays, pension, and so on. Use the information below to answer them.

Additional information about the post:	
Salary	£43,000 a year
Holidays	Six weeks
Company car	Yes
Pension	Company contributes 8.5%
Travel	Two-three months a year
Possible clients	Banks, Accountancy firms, Insurance companies

File 37

SEE PAGE 78

Student B

Your work for Flexible Software Ltd, providing computer equipment for companies in Europe. Your partner works for Eurodrive, a car hire company and wants to place an order with you. You need to negotiate the best deal possible with Eurodrive. Your boss made some suggestions below. Use his/her notes, and the conditions below, and discuss the sale with your partner.

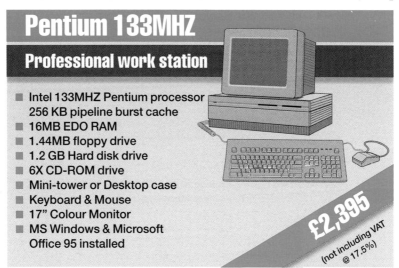

Pentium 133MHZ

Professional work station

- Intel 133MHZ Pentium processor 256 KB pipeline burst cache
- 16MB EDO RAM
- 1.44MB floppy drive
- 1.2 GB Hard disk drive
- 6X CD-ROM drive
- Mini-tower or Desktop case
- Keyboard & Mouse
- 17" Colour Monitor
- MS Windows & Microsoft Office 95 installed

£2,395 (not including VAT @ 17.5%)

Could you deliver ...?
How much ...?
That's a bit high.
Would you agree to ...?

Conditions (negotiable)

1 Terms of payment:

30 days/Cash on delivery: 3% discount

2 Delivery period: 3 weeks

3 Discounts: 26 to 50 units: 3.5%

51 units or more: 5%

4 Guarantee: One year on-site parts & labour warranty

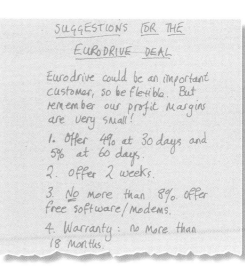

SUGGESTIONS FOR THE EURODRIVE DEAL

Eurodrive could be an important customer, so be flexible. But remember our profit margins are very small!

1. Offer 4% at 30 days and 5% at 60 days.

2. Offer 2 weeks.

3. No more than 8%. Offer free software/modems.

4. Warranty: no more than 18 months.

File 38

SEE PAGE 39

APG LTD | Annual Sales Conference

Venue	Park Lane Hotel, Carlton Room
Address	Old Park Lane, London W1V 9FL
Dates	Monday 15th to Wednesday 17th
Registration time	12.00 to 14.00

Monday	Opening speech	Peter Jackson
	Afternoon session	Listening to the Client
	Speaker	Lee Anaka

Tuesday	Morning session	European Sales Targets
	Speaker	Geneviève Leclerc
	Afternoon session	UK Sales Targets
	Speaker	John Pearson

Wednesday	Morning session	Distribution Problems
	Speaker	David Strong
	Afternoon session	Client Satisfaction
	Speaker	Susannah Peters

Times

Morning session
09.30 to 13.00

Afternoon session
14.15 to 17.00

Buffet Lunch

Every day
13.00 to 14.00

Buffet Dinner

Monday
18.00 to 19.00

Coffee Breaks

11.00 and 15.30

Social Events

Monday
Cocktail party

Tuesday
Conference dinner

File 39

SEE PAGE 18

Student B

1 You recently went to China on a business trip. You visited the Wuxi-Singapore Industrial Park. Answer your partner's questions. Use this information from the Internet to help you.

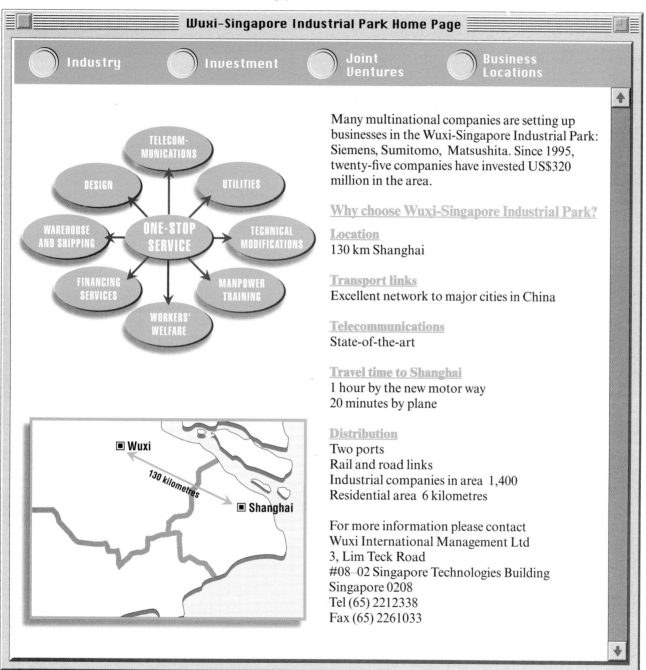

Wuxi-Singapore Industrial Park Home Page

Industry   Investment   Joint Ventures   Business Locations

ONE-STOP SERVICE
TELECOMMUNICATIONS
UTILITIES
TECHNICAL MODIFICATIONS
MANPOWER TRAINING
WORKERS' WELFARE
FINANCING SERVICES
WAREHOUSE AND SHIPPING
DESIGN

Many multinational companies are setting up businesses in the Wuxi-Singapore Industrial Park: Siemens, Sumitomo, Matsushita. Since 1995, twenty-five companies have invested US$320 million in the area.

Why choose Wuxi-Singapore Industrial Park?

Location
130 km Shanghai

Transport links
Excellent network to major cities in China

Telecommunications
State-of-the-art

Travel time to Shanghai
1 hour by the new motor way
20 minutes by plane

Distribution
Two ports
Rail and road links
Industrial companies in area 1,400
Residential area 6 kilometres

For more information please contact
Wuxi International Management Ltd
3, Lim Teck Road
#08–02 Singapore Technologies Building
Singapore 0208
Tel (65) 2212338
Fax (65) 2261033

■ Wuxi
130 kilometres
■ Shanghai

2 Discussion

What do you think are the priorities in setting up a new office? Make a list of the five most important things. Compare your list with your partner's.

File 40

SEE PAGE 26

Student B

Here are two different roles. Read the information and act out the conversations with your partner.

1 You work on the Customer Services Desk at Sydney airport, Australia. A traveller has a problem. Listen and try to solve it. Fill in the customer's details in the form below by asking questions.

CUSTOMER COMPLAINT

NAME

ADDRESS

TELEPHONE NUMBER

TRAVEL DETAILS

DESTINATION

DETAILS OF COMPLAINT

---

2 A travel agency booked the flight for your last trip to Poland. Look at the information below and make a formal complaint to the agency.

- Flight AE 345 Beijing - Moscow - Warsaw (change Moscow).
- The agency said you had an hour to make the connection.
- The plane arrived in Moscow on time.
- But the agency was wrong, you had only 20 minutes for the connecting flight to Warsaw.
- You missed an important meeting in Poland.
- You had to wait a day and spent the night in a hotel.

3 Do you have any similar stories to tell? Describe a bad experience you have had to your partner.

File 41

SEE PAGE 29

Student B

1 You are visiting your partner's company. You are free on Friday and Saturday and would like to go out with your colleague. Read the following information and make arrangements with him/her.

- You don't like fish very much.
- You don't like hotel restaurants.
- You don't like sport but you like museums and sightseeing.
- Your plane leaves early on Sunday morning so you want an early night.
- Next week is your daughter's birthday. You would like to buy a present on Saturday.
- Your partner is an important client, so be polite!

You could use some of the expressions in the box below.

> I prefer ...
> I'd like ...
> Perhaps we can ...
> Could we ...?

2 Now complete the following diary page with your arrangements for the weekend.

FRIDAY	SATURDAY	SUNDAY
		Drive to airport
		Flight BA 573
		Dep. 07.15

File 42

SEE PAGE 23

Student B

1 Read the statements about the British car-manufacturing company, Rolls-Royce. Choose the correct verbs from the box below and then complete the statements putting the verbs into the past tense.

> to die   to form   to rise   to build   to buy   to open   to make

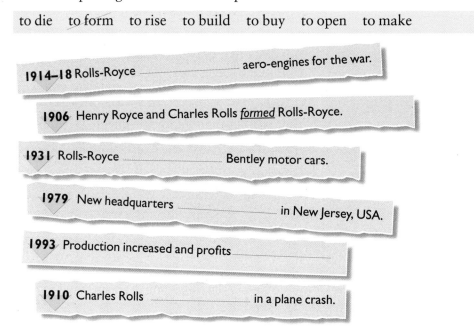

1914–18 Rolls-Royce _____ aero-engines for the war.

1906 Henry Royce and Charles Rolls _formed_ Rolls-Royce.

1931 Rolls-Royce _____ Bentley motor cars.

1979 New headquarters _____ in New Jersey, USA.

1993 Production increased and profits _____

1910 Charles Rolls _____ in a plane crash.

2 Now imagine you work for Rolls-Royce. You are preparing a presentation of the history of the company. Some of the information is in the wrong order. Exchange the information with your colleague and find the correct order. You both have different sentences.

Example   **B** *What happened first?*
          A *In 1904, Henry Royce made his first car.*
          B *And after that?*

3 Make notes in the table below. Then check the correct order in **Key 5.2** on page 110.

Year	What happened	Year	What happened
1 1904	Henry Royce made his first car.	7	
2		8	
3		9	
4		10	
5		11	
6		12	

4 Now practise giving the presentation with your colleague.

5 Do you know the history of another company? Tell your partner about it.

File 43

SEE PAGE 24

Student B

1 Your partner works for a market research company. He/she is researching the different kinds of holiday taken by business people and will ask you some questions. Look at the table below and invent information about your travel experiences. Make notes if you wish.

MARKET RESEARCH

HOLIDAY TRENDS IN BUSINESS

Company	
Position	
No. of holidays per year	
Last holiday	
When?	
Where?	
How long?	
Who with?	
Stayed at?	
Travelled by?	
Reasons for choice of holiday	
First time at this destination?	
Holiday good/bad/OK?	
Approx. costs	
Good value for money?	

2 Now change roles and imagine you work for the market research company, Consumer Profile Inc. Ask your partner questions using the table above. Make notes in the right hand column as you listen.

Example   *Good morning. I work for Consumer Profile, a market research company. I am researching the different kinds of holidays taken by business people.*

3 Imagine you are a market-researcher. What subjects interest you? Public transport? Sports shoes? CD Players? Choose a topic with your partner and carry out your own research.

File 44

SEE PAGE 54

Student B

I What is important for a good quality of life? Look at the map and the information below about three towns in Spain. The information comes from a Spanish newspaper. Some information is missing. Ask your partner questions to find out what it is.

Example   **A** *How many people live in Girona?*
             B *70,576.*

Quality of Life

	Palma	Girona	Vitoria
POPULATION	320,000		214,234
INHABITANTS PER SQUARE KM		1,839	7,651
GREEN (PARK) SPACE	2.5 m²	45m²	
MUNICIPAL BUDGET PER PERSON	$476		$1,099
AVERAGE SPEED OF TRAFFIC KM/HR	17.3	14.4	
KMS OF BICYCLE TRACK	8		30
PRICE OF A BUS TICKET		$0.73	$0.55
AVERAGE TEMPERATURE	18°C	14°C	
LEVEL OF NOISE		68 decibels	60 decibels
COST OF HOUSING PER M²	$764		$1,187
SPORT & CULTURE	4 concert halls 8 theatres 12 cinemas 26 libraries 2,613 restaurants 19 museums 27 Art galleries	5 radio stations 2 local newspapers 1 local television channel Private sports club	

2 Did you agree with the criterion on page 106? Do you have any different ideas? What is important to you? Write down your own list of criterion for a good quality of life.

1 _____

2 _____

3 _____

4 _____

5 _____

6 _____

7 _____

8 _____

9 _____

10 _____

3 Compare your list with your partner's. Do you have the same ideas? Now compare your list with the **Key 11.2**, on page 111.

4 Discussion

Does the town where you live offer a good quality of life? Discuss your town with your partner, or any other town that you like and know well.

File 45

SEE PAGE 60

Student B
Your partner is looking for some new offices. You have information about two possible locations. Describe the different locations to your partner. Help your partner to make a final decision about the best option when you finish.

Features	Overlee Business Estate	Belmont House
Space available	Single building 1,000m^2	750m^2 two floors
Cost	Rent £2,750 month 250m^2	£6,500 month
Distribution	Reception open plan	Reception area, 8 offices, 2 meeting rooms, open plan area
Distance city centre	25 km	3 km
Train station	10 minutes	5 minutes
Distance airport	45 minutes	45 minutes
Air-conditioning	Yes	No
Parking facilities	500 cars	10 cars
Special	3 restaurants, meeting room	Private garden

File 46

SEE PAGE 32

Student B

1 Read the article below about a company board meeting in Yorkshire, in the north of England.

MD says: 'Don't Forget Your Rucksack'!

It's the biggest boardroom in the world but there are no tables and no chairs. Larry Gould, Managing Director of the Link Up Group, holds his board meetings in the middle of the Yorkshire countryside.

It's a grey, wet morning in Yorkshire. A group of men and women are walking along a lake. They are laughing and joking. They are wearing boots and waterproof jackets. They look like tourists. But it is Monday, 9am, and they are talking business.

Larry Gould is leading the group. Link Up is a recruitment agency with a

turnover of £16 million a year. The others are the board directors and senior managers. This top Yorkshire company is holding a board meeting. Every three months they spend a morning in the countryside, discussing company issues. Gould is certain that these 'board walks' help his management staff to work better.

2 You are the Finance Director of a small manufacturing company. You read the article above in a business magazine and don't think it's a good idea. Make a list of what, in your opinion, are the advantages and disadvantages of this kind of board meeting.

Advantages	Disadvantages
good for morale	*expensive*
interesting	*waste of valuable time*

3 You don't want to introduce this kind of meeting into your company. Discuss the article with your Managing Director. Tell him/her your ideas, why you don't think outdoor meetings are a good idea, using some or all of the language in the box below. You must come to an agreement or a compromise.

What do you think ...?	I agree/disagree because ...
I think we should ...	Why don't we ...?
Shall we ...?	We could ...

4 Now compare your list of advantages and disadvantages with the list in **Key 7.1** on page 111.

Answer Key

Key 2.1

Student A

Student B

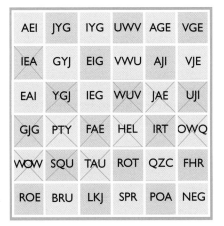

Key 2.3

Suggested answers.

A *Galaxy Computers*
B *Could I speak to Mr/Mrs/Ms Harris, please?*

A *Who's calling please?*
B *Michael Johnson.*
A *I'm sorry, could you repeat your name, please?*
B *Michael Johnson.*
A *I'm sorry, the line's engaged/busy. Will you hold?*
B *No thanks. Could you tell him, I called?*
A *Certainly, Mr Johnson.*

Key 2.4

Could you give me your VAT code number, please.

- Yes, of course. Just a minute. Ready?
- Yes, go ahead.
- It's TX34B. TX34B. Have you got that?
- Could I just read that back to you? TX34B.
- That's right. Anything else?
- No that's all. Bye.
- Bye.

Key 2.6

Xavier Allende
Salsa y Ache Havana Latin Disco
Tariq Nasir
Salsa y Ache Havana Latin Disco
Rosana Mendes
Salsa y Ache Havana Latin Disco
Cheng Weiqiang
The Playhouse
Heung Jyu
Salsa y Ache Havana Latin Disco
San Chi
Salsa y Ache Havana Latin Disco

Key 3.1

Suggested company profiles.

Apple Computer manufactures computers, software and printers. It has a 9% share of the personal computer market with net sales of approximately $10 million. It is a small company compared to Microsoft.

BASF is one of the world's top chemical companies. It produces over 8,000 products, but has been best known for its audio and video cassettes.

The BBC has an international network of radio transmitters. Worldwide, its radio broadcasts have more than 150 million listeners. It has two television channels in Britain.

Canon is a Japanese company and manufactures a wide range of electronic products such as cameras, printers, and photocopiers.

Eastman Kodak is a large American company with offices and factories all over the world. It offers photographic and digital imaging products and services. It is most famous for films and cameras.

ICI is a large multinational company based in London. It has factories all over the world. It manufactures paints, building materials, mining explosives, and industrial chemicals.

Kellogg's headquarters are in Michigan but the company earns over 40% of its annual revenues from outside the USA. It sells its products in 130 countries and has about half the European breakfast cereal market with leading brand names such as Rice Krispies, Kellogg's Corn Flakes, and Frosties.

Levi's The products from this company are famous all over the world. Teenagers love their advertisements. It is based in San Francisco and has revenues of over $6,000 million a year.

McDonald's Restaurants Ltd. is an American chain of fast food restaurants with outlets all over the world, including Moscow and Delhi.

Michelin produces tyres for a wide range of vehicles. It is the largest tyre company in the world with a 20% share of the world market. It also publishes road maps and tourist guides.

Microsoft produced the Windows operating system, famous worldwide. It is one of the largest computer companies in the world with annual sales of approximately $4,600 million.

Mitsubishi gives its name to 42 companies, all managed and financed separately. For example, Mitsubishi Motors, Mitsubishi Electric, Mitsubishi Bank, Nikon cameras, and Kirin beer.

Sony This is the world's leading manufacturer of electronic goods, for example, audio and video equipment, and televisions. It also has a record and a film company.

Key 3.2

1 I'm sorry, what time did you say?
2 I'm sorry, what day did you say?
3 I'm sorry, how many did you say?
4 I'm sorry, what hotel did you say?

5 I'm sorry, who did you say?
6 I'm sorry, how much did you say?
7 I'm sorry, how far/how many kilometres did you say?
8 I'm sorry, what did you say?

Key 4.2

1 Overhead projector
2 Roladex open file
3 Guillotine
4 Rubber stamp
5 Staple remover
6 Agenda letter tray

Key 5.1

1 How much was his company worth?
2 When was Walton born?
3 How did he pay for his studies?
4 How much money did he borrow to buy the franchise store?
5 When did he open the first Wal-mart discount store?
6 What could customers buy?
7 How many stores could Walton visit in the USA in a day?
8 Where was the network of stores based?
9 What did he study at university?
10 Who did he open his first discount store with?
11 Where did he open his first discount store?
12 Why did Walton succeed?
13 What did Walton learn how to do?
14 How many stores did he build/How large was Walton's network of discount stores?
15 How did he supply stores with fresh produce?
16 When did Walton die?/How old was Walton when he died?/At what age did he die?

Key 5.2

1 Henry Royce made his first car.
2 Henry Royce and Charles Rolls

formed Rolls-Royce.
3 Production expanded and relocated to Derby.
4 Charles Rolls died in a plane crash.
5 Rolls-Royce built aero engines for the war.
6 Rolls-Royce bought Bentley motor cars.
7 Sir Henry Royce died aged 70.
8 US subsidiary opened in New York.
9 Workforce increased to 5,000 employees.
10 New headquarters opened in New Jersey, USA.
11 Recession: company cut back production.
12 Production increased and profits rose.

Key 6.1

Suggested answers

1 Would you like a coffee?
2 Would you like to see the factory now?
3 Would you like to go out for dinner next week?
4 Would you like to play golf this weekend?
5 Would you like to go to the theatre after dinner?
6 Would you like to do some sightseeing on Tuesday?
7 Would you like to play golf on Saturday?
8 Would you like to see round the factory this afternoon?

Key 6.5

2 There are many possible answers.

1 Would you like to go to the theatre/cinema/a restaurant tonight?
2 I'm going to America next month.
3 I'm too busy to finish the report today.
4 Have a good weekend/holiday/trip.

5 Did the Managing Director like your presentation?

6 Would you like to go out for lunch?

Key 7.1

Advantages
Good for morale
Interesting
Healthy
Staff keep fit
Relaxing
Help staff to concentrate more
Reduces tension

Disadvantages
Expensive
Waste of time
Different to normal meetings
Not serious enough
Can't write
Like a holiday
Bad example to other staff
Impossible to concentrate

Key 8.1

The best time to arrange a meeting is Tuesday morning at about 11am.

Key 8.2

1	tied up	5	fix
2	suit	6	free
3	appointment	7	agenda
4	manage	8	cancel

Key 11.2

Some suggestions.

Level of unemployment
Parkland
Cost of housing
Income levels
Rate of inflation
Cultural activities
Quantity of traffic
Population
Bicycle tracks
Average temperatures
Number of cars
Noise levels

Quality of schooling
Quality of healthcare
Shopping facilities
Crime rates
Industry
Business opportunities
Distance from capital city
Transport facilities
Cost of living

Key 11.5

Suggested answers.

- Media advertising: television, radio, newspapers
- Sponsorship of sporting or cultural events
- Endorsement by popular national figures
- Billboards
- Trade fairs
- Advertisements in trade magazines
- Mailshots (junk mail)

Key 13.1

Suggested answer, but you may have a different order.

1 Arrive at airport
2 Check in
3 Wait for flight to be called
4 Go through passport control
5 Buy presents in duty-free shop
6 Go through metal detector
7 Go to boarding gate
8 Get on plane
9 Take off
10 Land
11 Go to arrivals terminal
12 Pass immigration control
13 Wait for luggage
14 Go through customs
15 Taxi to hotel

Key 14.1

1 Hello! Nice to see you again.
2 Hello, how are you?
3 I'm fine. Did you have a good journey?
4 Yes. Thanks for sending the driver.

5 Not at all. Shall we look around the factory now?
6 OK. Could I leave my bags here?
7 Of course. What do you think of new office?
8 It's very smart. When did you move in?
9 About 6 months ago. We needed more space.
10 So the business is doing well?
11 Yes. Sales have increased by 50% this year.
12 That's very good.
13 Here we are. Put this hard hat on and then we can go in.

Key 14.4

1 Ingredients
2 Ingredients mixed
3 Biscuits formed
4 Baked
5 Collated
6 Wrapped
7 Boxed by hand
8 Boxes sealed
9 Palletized

Key 15.1

1 If I were rich, I'd sail around the world.
2 If I won the lottery, I'd invest it in shares.
3 If I went on a training course, I'd know how the computer system works.
4 If they opened a new office, they'd need more staff.
5 If my boss gave me a pay rise, I'd take out a mortgage.
9 If I went to England for six months, I'd learn to speak good English.
10 If my boss resigned, I'd get his job.
6 If I made lots of money, I'd give it to charity.
7 If I had enough capital, I'd start my own company.
8 If I lost my job, I'd go back to university.